READER PRAISE

"An outstanding presentation . . . that is long overdue."

Pastor Kevin Lea's book is an outstanding presentation of a doctrinal matter that is long overdue for an open and Scripture-based discussion, for the sake of the body of Christ.

I truly believe that if this book were to get into the right hands, it has the potential to prod a much-needed reversal of the alarming trend toward Calvinism that is taking place today amongst our more conservative-minded brethren.

—DR. KERRY TRAHAN, *author, and founding pastor of A Church of Jesus [Est. 1983] in Port Neches, Texas*

"This small book is a much needed tool . . ."

In *Testing the Doctrine of Original Sin*, **Pastor Kevin Lea** clearly refutes the teachings of Augustine of Hippo, John Calvin and R.C. Sproul—by clarifying specific original Hebrew text, and the words of Christ.

This small book is a much needed tool in our ongoing ministry to share salvation through personal faith in the death, burial and resurrection of Jesus Christ to "whosoever believes".

—*GARY HARRIS, Layleader, San Antonio, Texas*

"Pure joy . . . We cannot wait to pass it on to others!"

After years of wandering in the wilderness, not even sure if I was saved, a relative suggested we listen to *Grace To You* with John MacArthur. My husband and I did—for countless hours. We also began to read books by R.C Sproul, Steve Lawson, A.W. Pink and others. We thought, "This is it—what we've been missing all along!" (Indeed, these teachings put a fear of the Lord into our hearts regarding His Holiness, which is *actually* what we had been missing.) However, we lacked discernment to understand that we were being taught a false belief system—one which *adds* to God's precious word and *distorts* the simplicity of the Gospel of Jesus Christ.

But after reading this book, I finally understand what a loving God and gracious and merciful Savior we have, Who loves us so much that *He gives us the choice* to believe in Him and His finished work on the Cross at Calvary. I know the creatures He created were NOT created to be destroyed, but to glorify Him and to praise Him for His salvation! *Every one of the Scripture references Pastor Kevin uses to tear down the "T" in the dreaded T.U.L.I.P. has been deliverance—and pure joy to read again and again!*

Thank you, Pastor Kevin, for your patience and kindness through this journey with us, and for this loving book that you've poured your heart into. *Without the "T," U.L.I.P. makes no sense at all. We are eternally grateful for the Truth, and cannot wait to pass it on to others!*

—JEFF & JANINE KROGH, Port Orchard, Washington

Does Calvinism's "Total Depravity"
Condemn the Preborn Infant?

TESTING
the Doctrine of
ORIGINAL SIN

A Biblical Response to the Reformed Theology of

R. C. SPROUL

Kevin Lea

TESTING THE DOCTRINE OF ORIGINAL SIN:
A Biblical Response to the Reformed Theology of R.C. Sproul

by Kevin Lea

Published by Soundview Media Group

Copyright ©2024 by Kevin Lea

ISBN 978-1-962311-00-7

Unless otherwise indicated, Scripture quotations are from
The Holy Bible, New King James Version (NKJV)

Soundview Media Group
Anderson Island, WA 98303

soundview.ministries@proton.me

Cover and Interior Design by Mark Dinsmore
MD Creative / emdeecreative@gmail.com

PRINTED IN THE UNITED STATES OF AMERICA

Dedication

I dedicate this booklet to my beloved wife of nearly fifty years, Juanita Lea, who has supported our ministry through thick and thin, kept my dinners warm, and so much more, with a patience and grace far beyond what I deserve. I love you Juanita.

Prologue

The impetus for this booklet began several years ago as a result of a conversation I had with a friend and former congregant. He and his wife had left the church that I pastor in order to attend a reformed/Calvinist church in our area.

During the conversation, he mentioned how he had been inspired by the writings of Augustine. I warned him about how his teachings had laid the foundation for the false doctrines of the Roman Catholic Church. The friend then asked me, "Well don't you believe in the doctrine of original sin?" I answered in the affirmative, which was followed by his quick response, "Well then, you believe in Augustine's teaching—the same as Calvinism."

When we concluded our conversation, I walked away confused—because I knew what I meant by original sin, but clearly it could not be the same thing as what Augustine/Calvin and my friend believed. This started my quest to understand the Calvinist's dictionary of words and terms and how they compared to Scripture and my understanding.

For example, the word sin is an archery term which means "to miss the mark." By application, it means failure to obey God's commands. In their curriculum to children, Child Evangelism Fellowship teaches that sin is "whatever you think, say or do that is contrary to God's law."

The word *original* can have many meanings. Put together, *original sin* to me meant that as a result of Adam's [original] sin, every one is destined to sin (miss the mark) against God.

But the Calvinist has a different dictionary. To them, *original sin* means that because of Adam's sin, all human souls originate, at conception, in a state of being a sinner. To them, the baby in the womb is already a sinner—and thus has missed the mark before even knowing what the mark is.

Simply put, to the non-Calvinist, we are born "to sin;" but to the Calvinist we are born "in sin"—and as readers will see in this volume, they use just one verse in the Bible to make this twist.

The confusion surrounding the term "original sin" is just one example of what is covered in this booklet. Words have meaning and thus it is important—even imperative—to understand how the terms and clichés used by Calvinists differ from biblical definitions, so that we can discern and speak the truth.

Satan twisted the meaning of God's first command when he deceived Eve in the Garden of Eden. God said the fruit of the tree of the knowledge of good and evil would bring death if eaten; while Satan told Eve that the fruit of the tree was a path to godhood. Same tree—different "dictionaries" and destinations.

Mormons will tell you that they believe in Jesus as their savior—and as proof, they emphasize that their church's name includes the name of Jesus. But we all know that the Jesus of the Mormons is not the Jesus of the Bible. (The Apostle Paul makes this abundantly clear in Galatians 1:6-9 and 2 Corinthians 11:3-4.)

In like manner, Calvinism twists the Word of God to create false meanings and thus teaches false doctrines. This is why I plan to give one of the first copies of this booklet to my Calvinist friend, and explain:

> After further study, I want to change my answer of years ago to, "No, the Bible does not teach the doctrine of Original Sin as espoused by Augustine and Calvinists, so I don't believe it—nor do I believe in the other tenets of Calvinism which are built upon their twisting of Psalm 51:5.

After reading this edition, dear reader, I hope that you will also embrace the biblical truths that caused me to change my answer—and that in the future your use of words will be based on scripture rather than man-made clichés.

Preface

Do preborn and infant babies go to heaven when they die? What about young children? Has God already determined who can be saved and who cannot? Do I have any choice in the matter? Or am I simply a pawn on God's chessboard of life and death? Why should I or anyone share the gospel, as Jesus commanded, if God has foreordained all our eternal destinies? Why, in Psalm 51:5, do some Bible versions clearly state that King David was conceived as a sinner and others do not? Is the statement, "We sin because we are sinners" biblical?

These questions, and many more, have divided the church for more than 500 years, ever since French Reformer John Calvin (10 July 1509 – 27 May 1564) promulgated his doctrines on election and predestination. So, did the Church lack accurate understanding of the Scriptures pertaining to salvation for 1500 years, waiting for Calvin to unlock the mysteries of God's grace? Or, rather, as I will demonstrate, do the tenets of Calvin's systematic theology actually redefine the character of God contrary to what is revealed in Holy Scripture?

In this booklet, I will briefly compare the doctrines of Calvin with the inspired Word of God in a way that I hope will be clear to Christians seeking answers to these questions. As my source on Calvinism, I refer to writings of one of its most respected apologists, the late Dr. Robert Charles (R.C.) Sproul (13 February 1939 – 14 December 2017).

About eight months before he died, Dr. Sproul summarized his position on the main tenets of Calvinism in articles posted on the website of Ligonier Ministries, which he founded (ligonier.org). These tenets, which were first developed during the Synod of Dort, 1618-1619, are:

Total Depravity (T); Unconditional Election (U); Limited Atonement (L); Irresistible Grace (I); and Perseverance of the Saints (P), often referred to collectively by the acronym TULIP. Note that the Canons of Calvinism, as issued by the Synod of Dort, were not in the exact order and wording above. In the years after Dort, the Reformers tweaked the wording and order until Cleland Boyd McAfee coined the acrostic TULIP in 1905.*

A Calvinist-leaning friend read an earlier draft of this booklet and commented that he was not impressed with R.C. Sproul's arguments. I responded that every Calvinist teacher I have ever heard or read uses these same arguments in their explanation of TULIP, which is why he should be unimpressed with Calvinist doctrine rather than one of its messengers.

This booklet will primarily deal with the cornerstone of Calvinism, which is Original Sin and Total Depravity, and then briefly conclude with an analysis of three of the other four tenets. I do not discuss Perseverance of the Saints, as the Bible is very clear that those who are truly saved will be still walking in the faith at the end:

> **Hebrews 3:14,15** *For we have become partakers of Christ if we hold the beginning of our confidence steadfast to the end, while it is said: "Today, if you will hear His voice, do not harden your hearts as in the rebellion."*

I pray this discussion will assist both those who are new to and those who are well familiar with the debate.

---

* William H. Vail's Five Points of Calvinism Historically Considered, https://www.logcollegepress.com/blog/2018/11/15/william-h-vails-five-points-of-calvinism-historically-considered.

Acknowledgements

After three decades as a senior pastor, I sensed it was the time to put in writing how I have responded to the hundreds of people who have over the decades asked (or lectured!) me about the role of election compared to free will in personal salvation.

My original goal was to prepare a brief article that accurately presented both sides of the debate and that could be understood by all sincere seekers of biblical truth. Achieving accuracy, clarity, and brevity proved to be a daunting task, and I wish to acknowledge the special people who helped bring this booklet to fruition.

Thank you to my longtime friend and Calvinist advocate Tom Malley, who helped ensure that my presentation of Calvinism as put forth in the writing of R.C. Sproul was accurate. Any inadvertent inaccuracies are my own, however.

Thank you to Jane Albright, word-smith extraordinaire, who mercilessly slashed extraneous words and skillfully re-worded my occasionally overly passionate language, diligently heeding my instruction to "take the Kevin out of 'Testing the Doctrine of Original Sin.'"

Special thanks to truth-lover, Bible student, and artistic genius Mark Dinsmore who created the layout and cover for this booklet and made many valuable editorial improvements as well.

Although I disagree with Pastor John MacArthur's position on Original Sin and related teachings, I want to thank him for his many verse-by-verse teachings from which I have learned much and for his biblical leadership during COVID.

Most importantly, I give all thanks and glory to our Lord Jesus Christ, "Who, desires all men to be saved and to come to the knowledge of the truth" (1 Timothy 2:4).

TABLE OF CONTENTS

Prologue vii

Preface ix

Acknowledgments xi

Introduction 1

Total Depravity 3
    Overview 3
    Does Psalm 51 Teach that Preborn and Young Children are Sinners? 5
    God's Word Contradicts the Doctrine of Original Sin 16
    Why are angels assigned to totally-depraved-from-conception little ones? 20
    An Aside – Does God Judge Children for the Sins of their Fathers? 21
    When / Why do We Sin? 22
    What is "Total Depravity" Anyway? 24
    Why do We Die Physically? 31
    The Scarlet Thread 35

Scripture Refutes the Unbiblical Doctrine of Total Depravity 37

Old Testament Verses	37
New Testament Verses	38

Summary 41
Total Depravity	41
Unconditional Election	41
Limited Atonement	58
Irresistible Grace	59

Closing Thoughts 61

Introduction

This booklet refers to the teachings of R.C. Sproul that at the following links:

1. Total Depravity. From R.C. Sproul Mar 25, 2017

    *https://www.ligonier.org/blog/
    tulip-and-reformed-theology-total-depravity/*

2. Unconditional Election. From R.C. Sproul Apr 01, 2017

    *https://www.ligonier.org/blog/
    tulip-and-reformed-theology-unconditional-election/*

3. Limited Atonement. From R.C. Sproul Apr 08, 2017

    https://www.ligonier.org/blog/
    tulip-and-reformed-theology-limited-atonement/

4. Irresistible Grace. From R.C. Sproul Apr 15, 2017

    https://www.ligonier.org/blog/
    tulip-and-reformed-theology-irresistible-grace/

Total Depravity

Note: I will first give key points from Dr. Sproul's web posting on Total Depravity, which are shaded with lines above and beneath. My response to each of his points, with relevant Scripture, is below.

Overview

> R.C. Sproul – "The doctrine of Total Depravity reflects the Reformed viewpoint of Original Sin. That term—Original Sin—is often misunderstood in the popular arena. Some people assume that the term Original Sin must refer to the first sin—the original transgression that we've all copied in many different ways in our own lives, that is, the first sin of Adam and Eve. But that's not what Original Sin has referred to historically in the church. Rather, the doctrine of Original Sin defines the consequences to the human race because of that first sin."

> R.C. Sproul — "Tweet this: WE ARE NOT SINNERS BECAUSE WE SIN. WE SIN BECAUSE WE ARE SINNERS. —R.C. SPROUL"

We will see that this is neither biblically accurate, nor has this historically been the view held by the Church. Calvinists will say that Original Sin is the change in nature from what God created Adam with (not a sinner) to what all humans have become after the fall (sinners), *starting at conception*. A Calvinist friend of mine says, "Original Sin is the fallen nature of man, not the imputation of Adam's sin." But if those born after Adam are born "sinners" as R.C. Sproul says, then what was it that imputed sin to them? If not being imputed as a result of Adam's sin, how did the conceived baby in the womb get tagged with being a sinner before he/she could commit a sin against God?

> R.C. Sproul – "Virtually every church historically that has a creed or a confession has agreed that something very serious happened to the human race as a result of the first sin—that first sin resulted in Original Sin."

> R.C. Sproul – "That is, as a result of the sin of Adam and Eve, the entire human race fell, and our nature as human beings since the fall has been influenced by the power of evil."

The Bible is indisputably clear that things changed on the day that Adam ate from the Tree of the Knowledge of Good and Evil, when he ingested a spiritual poison and thus brought sin into the world. On that day, man died, not physically, but spiritually as it pertained to his relationship with God. Once in perfect fellowship with his Creator, Adam was now ashamed, and he hid from God. He now had to work by the sweat of his brow. The woman is now to be ruled over by her husband and suffer the pain of childbirth (Genesis 3). Creation suffered the consequences of man's sin also, being placed into a bondage that will last until the Second Coming of Jesus Christ (Romans 8:18-22).

I will be making the case throughout this rebuttal that what we inherited from Adam was *rebellion*, not sin. Mankind's nature is now self-willed, determined to decide for himself what is good and evil. Adam's original rebellion against God's single law was passed down to all generations after him, infecting humanity with a spirit of rebellion against all authority. From the time that we are old enough to understand what we are told to do, we obey only if and when we decide to. First, we rebel against our parents, then against any outside authority, and then, when we discover what God has commanded us to do, we join Adam in rebelling against our Creator as well, which at that moment makes us a sinner in the eyes of God.

But is the single-celled, just-conceived human being able to rebel against God in any way? What about a baby just about to enter the world nine months later? Or when he/she doesn't even know how to speak, crawl, understand, or talk? Calvinists teach that just-conceived and young children all have a "sin nature" as a result of what Adam did as an adult when he disobeyed God (performing the actual act of sin). Are these preborn and infant children going to be judged as sinners if they die? We will examine this question further until we reach a biblical answer.

Does Psalm 51 Teach that Preborn and Young Children are Sinners?

Calvinists use a single verse, Psalm 51:5, as their predominant proof text in support of the doctrines of Original Sin and Total Depravity. In the following pages, I point out that in some Bibles, Psalm 51:5 clearly states that King David considered that he was a sinner from the moment he was conceived; yet other Bibles are not so clear, leaving open other possible interpretations. Before jumping into why this is so, I will summarize this history of our modern Bible translations.

Biblical Christians believe that God used the authors of the books of the Bible to pen the very "God-breathed" (inspired) words contained in the Old and New Testament (2 Peter 1:19-21). With some exceptions, God inspired these texts to be written in the Hebrew language for the Old Testament, and Greek for the New.

Throughout history, men have taken manuscripts that were written or copied in the original languages to translate the Holy Word of God into other languages. Until recently, great care was taken by translators to maintain the exact word-for-word meaning.

Several decades ago, Bible translators and publishers began to produce paraphrased Bibles that would be easier for modern readers to understand. These translators used their own words and sentence structure to simplify the language while still conveying what *they thought* God intended to communicate in the original inspired text. These various paraphrase versions of the Bible were marketed as Thought-for-Thought, Dynamic Equivalent, Optimal Equivalence, etc.

The result of this shift away from word-for-word translations paved the way for "scholars" to phrase the text in such a way that it supported their doctrinal bias, thus corrupting the text. Some publishers welcomed these same scholars to further promote their doctrinal bias in the marginal notes associated with study bibles. We will see that this is certainly the case as it pertains to Psalm 51:5.

> R.C. Sproul – "As David declared in the Old Testament, 'Oh, God, I was born in sin, and in sin did my mother conceive me'" Psalm 51:5.

Sproul does not cite the Bible version that he used, though the verse reference hyperlinks to the English Standard Version (ESV). However, he does not quote this version accurately. Additionally, none of the 28 English versions that I have are worded as he quotes. Neither does the Hebrew text read as Sproul states above. This example illustrates that believers, as Bible students, must be wary of doctrines espoused by people *who change the biblical text to support their theological bias.*

> R.C. Sproul – "He was not saying that it was sinful for his mother to have borne children; neither was he saying that he had done something evil by being born. Rather, he was acknowledging the human condition of fallenness—that condition that was part of the experience of his parents, a condition that he himself brought into this world. Therefore, Original Sin has to do with the fallen nature of mankind."

Original Sin and Fallen Nature have very different meanings. The idea of a fallen or rebellious nature does not impute sin at conception; Original Sin as defined by Calvinists does. The distinction becomes clear as we take a look at Psalm 51:5, the Scripture passage that Sproul uses as his proof text for Original Sin. Note the comparison of this verse between several **word-for-word translations** from the Hebrew, and **paraphrase versions** of the Bible, which incorporate man's interpretation of the inspired text:

> **English Standard Version (ESV):** *Behold, I was brought forth in iniquity, and in sin did my mother conceive me.*

Please note how this verse does not read the same as Sproul quotes on page 6 and at his website with a link that *says* it goes to the ESV.

> **King James:** *Behold, I was shapen in iniquity; and in sin did my mother conceive me.*
>
> **New King James:** *Behold, I was brought forth in iniquity, and in sin my mother conceived me.*
>
> **New American Standard:** *Behold, I was brought forth in iniquity, and in sin my mother conceived me.*
>
> **Septuagint:** *For, behold, I was conceived in iniquities, and in sins* [plural] *did my mother conceive me.*

The true word-for-word translations of ESV, KJV, NKJV, NAS, and Septuagint could easily be interpreted to mean that it was David's mother who was committing some unspecified sins in the act of his conception. Or it could mean simply that she was a sinful woman when she conceived and now David is a sinful man confessing to God his sin, which was a result of his inherited desire to rebel, thus causing him to become "shapen in iniquity."

Here are some paraphrases, not word-for-word translations, which could be interpreted in a way that would support R.C. Sproul's position that David considered himself a sinner at conception:

> **Amplified:** *Behold, I was brought forth in [a state of] iniquity; my mother was sinful who conceived me [and I too am sinful].* [John 3:6; Romans 5:12; Ephesians 2:3.]
>
> **New International Version:** *Surely I was sinful at birth, sinful from the time my mother conceived me.*
>
> **New Living Translation:** *For I was born a sinner— yes, from the moment my mother conceived me.*
>
> **Good News Translation:** *I have been evil from the day I was born; from the time I was conceived, I have been sinful.*
>
> **The Living Bible:** *But I was born a sinner, yes, from the moment my mother conceived me.*
>
> **THE MESSAGE (by Eugene H. Peterson):** *I've been out of step with you for a long time, in the wrong since before I was born.*

Notice how modern publishers have added words that do not exist in the original inspired Hebrew text—and have done so in a way to support a doctrine that did not exist in the church until Augustine of Hippo first proposed it in about AD 400. Further, there is no other verse in the entire Bible that supports the idea that the single cell of a just-conceived new life is a sinner because of Adam's sin.

The Church of Jesus Christ of Latter-Day Saints believes that a dead person can be baptized by proxy based on one verse from

1 Corinthians 15:29, *"Otherwise, what will they do who are baptized for the dead, if the dead do not rise at all? Why then are they baptized for the dead?"*

But the true Christian church knows that this one verse is twisted by the Mormons to support their false teachings; the rest of Scripture and the gospel itself refute this false doctrine. In the same way, Calvinists use a single verse, Psalm 51:5, as the basis for their doctrine of Total Depravity. Standard rules of biblical interpretation warn against basing doctrine on a single verse of Scripture—especially if, in the Calvinist's case, the verse is corrupted in popular paraphrase versions in a way that differs from the original, inspired text.

Although the ESV is an accurate translation of the Hebrew for this verse, the ESV Study Bible note for Psalm 51:5 twists the passage in the same way as the paraphrases above. In the 2016 printing of this study Bible,* the note reads (with bolding in the original):

> **I was brought forth** *(that is, from the womb)* **in iniquity.** *David thinks of himself as a sinful person from the time of his birth.* **in (sic) sin did my mother conceive me.** *This idea is not that the act of conception was itself sinful, but as the parallel first line shows [Romans 5:12] that each worshiper learns to trace his sinful tendencies to the very beginning of his existence – not only from birth but even before that, to conception. (This certainly attributes moral accountability, the most important aspect of "personhood," to the developing baby in the womb. This is why many see this passage as implying that an unborn child should be thought of as a human person from the point of conception in his mother's womb.)*

The ESV study Bible and others make reference to the following verses as parallel passages—which they claim support the idea of "Original Sin"—but as you can tell by reading actual word-for-word translations, they do not:

---

* Published by Crossway, ESV Permanent Text Edition (2016)

> **Romans 5:12** *Therefore, just as through one man sin entered the world* [when the man Adam sinned against God], *and death through sin, and thus death spread to all men, because all sinned.*

Yes, history has proven that all men, in their rebellious fallen nature, eventually sin against God, but that does not mean that the single-cell baby David, in the womb of his mother, was a sinner in the eyes of God.

> **Romans 5:19** *For as by one man's disobedience many were made sinners, so also by one Man's obedience many will be made righteous.*

Yes many [men] have become sinners in their rebellion. The Bible teaches that *"All [men] have sinned and have fallen short of the glory of God"* (Romans 3:23).

Yes, I just added the clarifying word "men" to the Romans 3:23 text above—so am I guilty of what I accused the above publishers of various Bible paraphrases? No; because, according to the Bible, sinning against God requires that one must know that there is a God (spiritual knowledge), know what He commands (moral knowledge), and deliberate disobedience (moral transgression). In other words, sinning takes deliberate, conscious disobedience against God, something adults do, but of which a baby is not capable.

> **Ephesians 2:1-3** *And you* [the adults reading Paul's epistle] *He made alive, who were dead in trespasses and sins, in which you once walked according to the course of this world, according to the prince of the power of the air, the spirit who now works in the sons of disobedience, among whom also we all once conducted ourselves in the lusts of our flesh, fulfilling the desires of the flesh and of the mind, and were by nature children of wrath, just as the others.*

This verse has nothing to do with "Original Sin" as espoused by R.C. Sproul. These verses speak of adults who once walked in lustful sins against God and thus were children of wrath.

> **Job 14:1-4** *Man, who is born of woman is of few days and full of trouble. He comes forth like a flower and fades away; he flees like a shadow and does not continue. And do You open Your eyes on such a one, and bring me to judgment with Yourself? Who can bring a clean thing out of an unclean? No one!*

Calvinists use the phrase, *"Who can bring a clean thing out of an unclean"* as a support for the doctrine of "Original Sin." However, it is perfectly clear from the context that Job is speaking of an adult, not a baby in the womb.

> **Job 15:14** *What is man, that he could be pure? And he who is born of a woman, that he could be righteous?*

Again, the context implies that no adult human can be righteous. This verse is not speaking of Original Sin as Calvinists define it.

There is one more Bible paraphrase that needs to be addressed. The Holman Christian Standard Bible (HCSB) uses the "Optimal Equivalent," rather than word-for-word, method of translating.

From the HCSB (emphasis mine):

> "Optimal equivalence starts with an exhaustive analysis of the text at every level (word, phrase, clause sentence, discourse) in the original meaning and intention (or purpose). **Then relying on the latest and best tools and experts, the nearest corresponding semantic and linguistic equivalents are used to convey as much of the information and intention of the original text with as much clarity and readability as possible.** This process assures the maximum transfer of both the words **and thoughts** contained in the original. The HCSB uses optimal equivalence as its translation philosophy. When a literal translation meets these criteria, it is used. **When clarity and readability demand an idiomatic**

translation, the reader can still access the form of the original text by means of a footnote with the abbreviation "Lit."

HCSB's "Optimal Equivalent" of Psalm 51:5:

Indeed, I was guilty when I was born; I was sinful when my mother conceived me.

The HCSB note on Psalm 51:5 states,

"This verse has prompted a variety of interpretations. Some have interpreted it to mean that marriage and childbearing are a curse; this is untenable in light of the rest of Scripture (Psalm 127:3; Hebrews 13:4)."

But this note does not address that David's mother could have been in sin by violating the law of uncleanness, or even having conceived out of wedlock—or both, since the Septuagint states "sins" (plural). What if his mother was single and not betrothed when David was conceived? If so, his parents would have been "in sin" and required by the law to marry (Deuteronomy 22:28,29). Could it be that David was conceived outside of marriage by a woman other than the mother of Jesse's other sons? Perhaps this was why his father did not initially include him with his older brothers when Samuel came to anoint one of them to be the future king (1 Samuel 16).

Could this also be the reason that David's eldest brother Eliab mocked him when David came into the Israelite army during the battle with Goliath (1 Samuel 17:28)? We cannot know for sure, but it is certainly plausible and would help explain David's father's and his brother's treatment of him. What if this was the reason David used this Hebrew wording in his prayer and was in no way trying to promote the Calvinist concept of Original Sin and the related Total Depravity?

> HCSB: "Another interpretation is that this refers to a specific sin. Perhaps adultery, committed by David's mother, but there is no evidence of this in the biblical text."

This is an argument of silence, which is very weak considering the subject. What if David had been conceived in an act of adultery between Jesse and a married woman and this is what David meant by, "*in sin my mother conceived me?*" The Calvinist will say that this could not be what David meant because the Law of Moses required both adulterers be stoned to death, and Jesse was still alive in the historical narrative of David's later life (for example, 1 Samuel 16). However, the death penalty was not always carried out in ancient Israel, and clearly, David himself was spared stoning after his own adulterous relationship with Bathsheba (2 Samuel 11).

Therefore—though conjecture—I assert it *is* possible that his parents' adultery is what David was alluding to in Psalm 51:5—and if so, this also sheds light on David's behavior when his first son with Bathsheba, who was conceived in adultery, was dying (2 Samuel 12:16-22). In summary, while Calvinists say the *only* possible interpretation of David's statement is the doctrine of Original Sin, we see that is simply not true.

> HCSB: "Others connect this verse with ceremonial uncleanness in childbirth (Leviticus 12:2, 5; 15:18) but this is not the same as sin."

However, violation of the laws in the verses below *are* sin—any of which could have been associated with what David was referring:

> **Leviticus 15:19** *If a woman has a discharge, and the discharge from her body is blood, she shall be set apart seven days; and whoever touches her shall be unclean until evening.*

> **Leviticus 18:19** *Also you shall not approach a woman to uncover her nakedness as long as she is in her customary impurity.*

> **Deuteronomy 22:28,29** *If a man finds a young woman who is a virgin, who is not betrothed, and he seizes her and lies with her,*

and they are found out, then the man who lay with her shall give to the young woman's father fifty shekels of silver, and she shall be his wife because he has humbled her; he shall not be permitted to divorce her all his days.

The HCSB goes on to suggest that the prevalence of the Calvinist view is evidence of its veracity:

> HCSB: "Some say David is using rhetorical overstatement to describe his sinfulness. One of the most common interpretations in Christian history is that this verse teaches the doctrine of Original Sin."

More accurately, no one taught this view of Original Sin until Augustine of Hippo (November 13, 354 – August 28, 430), a North African theologian, formulated it after his professed conversion to Christianity (Augustine, *Confessions* 8:12). In fact, Augustine can be considered the father of Calvinist doctrine because he was also the first to formulate the doctrines of predestination (the divine foreordaining of all that will ever happen) and efficacious grace (the idea that God's salvation is granted to a fixed number of those whom He has already determined to save). Augustine also initiated infant baptism, intended to ensure a "chosen" child would go to heaven. The Bible does not teach these doctrines; they were invented by Augustine, a man.

> HCSB: "While not aiming to strictly identify the origin of human sinfulness with events at biological conception, David recognizes that sin pervades humankind as a universal condition from the very outset of our existence."

But this is *exactly* what the wording of Psalm 51:5 (in HCSB) R.C. Sproul is "aiming to identify." That human sinfulness originates at conception is the foundation of the Calvinist premise and their interpretation of Psalm 51. The Calvinist writers of this note in the HCSB are being disingenuous in trying to deflect the objections of people who cannot agree that humans are sinners from the moment of conception.

> HCSB: "Sin is everywhere and in everyone, and David confessed that it had been with him since birth."

Notice the switch in language from "conception" to "birth." In either case, the accurate, word-for-word translation of Psalm 51:5 does not teach what the Calvinist commentators of the HCSB propose—that David confessed he was a sinner from conception/birth.

> HCSB: "Far from forming the basis of an excuse (i.e., 'Why should I be blamed for my sins when I was born this way?') David's confession contrasts the 'blameless' (Psalm 51:4) ways of God with the innately evil ways of men."

But in Psalm 51, David is speaking as a grown man, not a just-conceived baby in the womb. He knows that he had violated the laws of God, which is sin, something a baby at conception, birth, or in infancy, cannot commit. Even a young child, who does not (yet) have any concept or awareness of God and His commandments cannot be considered guilty of sinning against God.

> **Psalm 51:4** *Against You, You only, have I sinned, and done this evil in Your sight — That You may be found just when You speak, and blameless when You judge.*

David knew that God was blameless to judge him for his evil sins of adultery and murder. But Calvinists want to say that God is also blameless to judge David, and all human beings, as sinners from the moment they are conceived in the womb. Their definitions of Original Sin and Total Depravity are the foundation of three other tenets of Calvinism. If man is not conceived a sinner in the womb, then there is no need or place for Unconditional Election, Limited Atonement, or Irresistible Grace. In addition, the Calvinist definition of Total Depravity is contrary to God's nature as reflected in His law.

God's Word Contradicts the Doctrine of Original Sin

Deuteronomy 24:16 *Fathers shall not be put to death for their children, nor shall children be put to death for their fathers; a person shall be put to death for his own sin.*

God would be breaking His own law if He were to judge children (of Adam) as sinners (requiring spiritual death) for Adam's sin. Ezekiel Chapter 18 also reveals that God judges individuals as sinners if and when they have consciously and individually broken His law.

Ezekiel 18:19-23; 31,32 *"Yet you say, 'Why should the son not bear the guilt of the father?' Because the son has done what is lawful and right, and has kept all My statutes and observed them, he shall surely live. The soul who sins shall die. The son shall not bear the guilt of the father, nor the father bear the guilt of the son. The righteousness of the righteous shall be upon himself, and the wickedness of the wicked shall be upon himself.*

"But if a wicked man turns from all his sins which he has committed, keeps all My statutes, and does what is lawful and right, he shall surely live; he shall not die. None of the transgressions which he has committed shall be remembered against him; because of the righteousness which he has done, he shall live. Do I have any pleasure at all that the wicked should die?" says the Lord God, "and not that he should turn from his ways and live? --- Cast away from you all the transgressions which you have committed, and get yourselves a new heart and a new spirit. For why should you die, O house of Israel? For I have no pleasure in the death of one who dies," says the Lord God. "Therefore turn and live!"

Even Paul teaches that a person is not a sinner (and therefore spiritually dead) until their own rebellious nature actually acts against God's law:

Romans 7:7-12 *What shall we say then? Is the law sin? Certainly not! On the contrary, I would not have **known** sin except through*

> the law. For I would not have known covetousness unless the law had said, "You shall not covet." But sin, taking opportunity by the commandment, produced in me all manner of evil desire. For apart from the law sin was dead. **I was alive** once without the law, but when the commandment came, sin revived and I died **[spiritually]**. And the commandment, which was to bring life, I found to **bring death.** For sin, taking occasion by the commandment, deceived me, and by it killed me. Therefore, the law is holy, and the commandment holy and just and good.

Paul was trained by the best of the scribes and Pharisees/rabbis of his day. He knew he was not condemned at conception. Rather, he believed that he was spiritually alive until he reached an age at which he became aware that his rebellious nature had caused him to sin against God. At that point, Paul states, under inspiration from God, that "he died" (spiritually).

James, under inspiration, reinforces Paul when he says that spiritual death comes when man gives into his rebellious desires, thus sinning against God:

> **James 1:14,15** But each one is tempted when he is drawn away by his own desires and enticed. Then, when desire has conceived, it gives birth to sin; and sin, when it is full-grown, brings forth death.

But what about Romans Chapter 1? Romans 1 teaches that Gentiles (who did not have the Mosaic law) are condemned or judged by God.

> **Romans 1:18-23** For the wrath of God is revealed from heaven against all ungodliness and unrighteousness of men, who suppress the truth in unrighteousness, because what may be known of God is manifest in them, for God has shown it to them. For since the creation of the world His invisible attributes are clearly seen, being understood by the things that are made, even His eternal power and Godhead, so that they are without excuse, because, although they knew God, they did not glorify Him as

> God, nor were thankful, but became futile in their thoughts, and their foolish hearts were darkened. Professing to be wise, they became fools, and changed the glory of the incorruptible God into an image made like corruptible man — and birds and four-footed animals and creeping things.

In these verses, we see that God reveals Himself to the Gentiles through the creation. When a person reaches the age where he is able to contemplate the creation and its wonder, God manifests His invisible attributes to him. Man is now at a crossroads. He either humbles himself and worships the Creator or succumbs to his rebellious nature, rejects God's authority, and ends up worshiping the creation instead of the Creator. At this point, the person has sinned against God, even without the Mosaic law. Paul then teaches what happens when a Gentile humbles himself.

> **Romans 2:14-16** *For when Gentiles, who do not have the law, by nature do the things in the law, these, although not having the law, are a law to themselves, who show the work of the law written in their hearts, their conscience also bearing witness, and between themselves their thoughts accusing or else excusing them in the day when God will judge the secrets of men by Jesus Christ, according to my gospel.*

As we see, these texts describe Gentiles who have reached the age of moral conscience. Paul is demonstrating that Jews and Gentiles alike are accountable to a Holy God, the context implying he is speaking of adults. He is not putting forth an argument for Original Sin and Total Depravity!

Many other portions of Scripture imply that children and even young adults are not condemned sinners in the eyes of God, for example:

> **Numbers 14:27-29** *"How long shall I bear with this evil congregation who complain against Me? I have heard the complaints which the children of Israel make against Me. Say to them, 'As I live,' says the Lord, 'just as you have spoken in My hearing,*

so I will do to you: The carcasses of you who have complained against Me shall fall in this wilderness, all of you who were numbered, according to your entire number, from twenty years old and above.'"

Deuteronomy 1:34-39 *"And the Lord heard the sound of your words, and was angry, and took an oath, saying, 'Surely not one of these men of this evil generation shall see that good land of which I swore to give to your fathers, except Caleb the son of Jephunneh; he shall see it, and to him and his children I am giving the land on which he walked, because he wholly followed the Lord.' The Lord was also angry with me for your sakes, saying, 'Even you shall not go in there. Joshua the son of Nun, who stands before you, he shall go in there. Encourage him, for he shall cause Israel to inherit it. 'Moreover your little ones and your children, who you say will be victims, **who today have no knowledge of good and evil,** they shall go in there; to them I will give it, and they shall possess it.'"*

We see that God spares those younger than 20 years of age from His punishment of the adult Israelites for their rebellion against God during the exodus from Egypt. Even today, neither society nor our legal system holds young children accountable for crimes such as shoplifting. Common sense says we do not arrest toddlers for grabbing a candy bar from the display while waiting in the checkout line! But Calvinists don't just lock them up; they condemn them to death row from the moment of conception.

2 Samuel 12:22,23 *And he said, "While the child was alive, I fasted and wept; for I said, 'Who can tell whether the Lord will be gracious to me, that the child may live?' But now he is dead; why should I fast? Can I bring him back again? I shall go to him, but he shall not return to me."*

King David knew that he would someday die and go be with his son. David has been forgiven by God and will at death be going to the bosom of Abraham, the comforted side of Hades (Luke 16:19-31), where he knew that his son would be as well.

> **Jonah 4:11** *"And should I not pity Nineveh, that great city, in which are more than one hundred and twenty thousand persons who cannot discern between their right hand and their left — and much livestock?"*

God reasons with Jonah that if His judgment falls upon Nineveh, one hundred and twenty thousand babies and toddlers are going to perish, along with much livestock. By implication, God views them as innocent and undeserving of His judgment on the adult population.

> **Matthew 18:10** *"Take heed that you do not despise one of these little ones, for I say to you that in heaven their angels always see the face of My Father who is in heaven."*

> **Hebrews 1:13,14** *But to which of the angels has He ever said: "Sit at My right hand, till I make Your enemies Your footstool?" Are they not all ministering spirits sent forth to minister for those who will inherit salvation?*

> **Matthew 19:13,14** *Then little children were brought to Him that He might put His hands on them and pray, but the disciples rebuked them. But Jesus said, "Let the little children come to Me, and do not forbid them; for of such is the kingdom of heaven."*

Why are angels assigned to totally-depraved-from-conception little ones?

In Hebrews 1:13,14, the Bible teaches that angels are sent forth to minister to those who will inherit salvation. Jesus says that little ones have angels, which must mean that at this time in their life—a time of innocence—God does not consider them to be sinners.

> **Mark 4:39-41** *When He came in, He said to them, "Why make this commotion and weep? The child is not dead, but sleeping." And they ridiculed Him. But when He had put them all outside, He took the father and the mother of the child, and those who were with Him, and entered where the child was lying. Then He took*

the child by the hand, and said to her, "Talitha, cumi," which is translated, "Little girl, I say to you, arise."

Jesus uses the term "sleeping" here and in John 11:11 to mean the person is physically dead but not spiritually dead. Therefore Jesus did not consider the ruler of the synagogue's twelve-year-old daughter to be dead in her trespasses and sins.

An Aside – Does God Judge Children for the Sins of their Fathers?

Some argue that the second of the Ten Commandments teaches that God judges children for the sins of their fathers:

> **Exodus 20:4-6** *You shall not make for yourself a carved image — any likeness of anything that is in heaven above, or that is in the earth beneath, or that is in the water under the earth; you shall not bow down to them nor serve them. For I, the Lord your God, am a jealous God, visiting the iniquity of the fathers upon the children to the third and fourth generations of those who hate Me, but showing mercy to thousands, to those who love Me and keep My commandments.*

Respected Bible commentator Adam Clarke (1762-1832) addresses this in his note on Exodus 20, verse 5:

> This necessarily implies—IF the children walk in the steps of their fathers, for no man can be condemned by divine justice for a crime of which he was never guilty; see Ezekiel 18. Idolatry is however particularly intended and visiting sins of this kind refers principally to national judgments. By withdrawing the divine protection, the idolatrous Israelites were delivered up into the hands of their enemies, from whom the gods in whom they had trusted could not deliver them. This God did to the third and fourth generations, i.e., successively; as may be seen in every part of the Jewish history, and particularly in the book of Judges. And this, at last, became the grand and the only effectual and lasting means

in his hand of their final deliverance from idolatry for it is well known that after the Babylonish captivity the Israelites were so completely saved from idolatry, as never more to have disgraced themselves by it as they had formerly done. These national judgments, thus continued from generation to generation, appear to be what are designed by the words in the text, "visiting the sins of the fathers upon the children, etc." *(from Adam Clarke's Commentary, Electronic Database. Copyright © 1996, 2003, 2005, 2006 by Biblesoft, Inc. All rights reserved.)*

As stated earlier, this verse also applies:

> **Deuteronomy 24:16** *Fathers shall not be put to death for their children, nor shall children be put to death for their fathers; a person shall be put to death for his own sin.*

When / Why do We Sin?

> R.C. Sproul – "The idea is that we are not sinners because we sin, but that we sin because we are sinners."

Romans 7:7-12 (cited earlier) clearly teaches that we are rebellious by nature and *become* sinners once we are old enough to be morally culpable (likely different ages for different people). A baby is not born a *sinner*; rather, he/she is born with a fallen nature—a *rebellious spirit*—and exhibits his/her rebellion against authority at a very early age. Once young people are old enough to *consciously* rebel against God, they reap the wages of sin, which is spiritual death. This penalty remains in effect until and unless they repent by calling upon the name of the Lord for forgiveness and receive the gift of God through faith in the saving work of Jesus Christ at Calvary (Romans 6:23; Luke 23:33).

Consider the words of Jesus Himself about the man born blind:

John 9:1,2 *Now as Jesus passed by, He saw a man who was blind from birth. And His disciples asked Him, saying, "Rabbi, who sinned, this man or his parents, that he was born blind?"*

Many in Jesus' day (and today) think that bad things only happen to bad/sinful people. We see this attitude expressed in the disciples' question. Being Jews under the law, they would have wanted to reject the notion that the young man's blindness was a punishment resulting from the parent's sin because that would contradict the law of God (Deuteronomy 24:16, Ezekiel 18). To them, the only other option was that God judged the baby in the womb for being sinful, and thus the question to Jesus. If the Jews had believed in Sproul's definition of Original Sin based on Psalm 51:5, there would have been no debate.

Consistent Calvinists could argue that the man was born blind because God sees him as a sinner and thus the child deserves whatever judgment God wants to place on him. The man's blindness, they would argue, is not a blot on God's character; rather, God is glorified in His mercy and grace because He does not cause all children to be born blind—which He could have been just in doing, because babies are all sinners. See *https://www.bible.ca/cal-T-consequences.htm* for writings of Calvinist apologists who teach that "unelected" babies who die are in hell.

Jesus then heals the blind man on the Sabbath. When the Pharisees interrogated the man, he gave glory to God for what Jesus had done to open his eyes and replied, *"If this Man were not from God, He could do nothing"* (John 9:33), to which the Pharisees indignantly retorted, *"You were completely **born in sins**, and are you teaching us"* (John 9:34)?

As we see, the Pharisees' accusations against the man agree with and predate Augustine's and Calvin's doctrine of Original Sin. But recall that Jesus had previously rebuked these religious leaders, telling them *"You are from your father, the devil"* (John 8:44).

But in contrast to the Pharisees' demonic doctrine of Original Sin, notice Jesus' response to his disciples' original question concerning the blind man:

> **John 9:3** *Jesus answered, "Neither this man nor his parents sinned, but that the works of God should be revealed in him."*

If the doctrine of Original Sin were true, this was the perfect opportunity for Jesus to expound on it, but He didn't. Jesus said the man's blindness was not a result of his or his parents' sin (meaning Jesus Himself said the blind man was not a sinner in the womb). The reason God chose this man to be born blind was because the blind man was destined to be a powerful example of God's power to heal in a way never done before and to show the difference between the proud and humble. The proud are spiritually blind; the humble receive spiritual sight to believe.

> **John 9:40,41** *Then some of the Pharisees who were with Him heard these words, and said to Him, "Are we blind also?" Jesus said to them, "If you were blind, you would have no sin; but now you say, 'We see.' Therefore your sin remains."*

What is "Total Depravity" Anyway?

> R.C. Sproul – "In the Reformed tradition, Total Depravity does not mean utter depravity. We often use the term total as a synonym for utter or for completely, so the notion of Total Depravity conjures up the idea that every human being is as bad as that person could possibly be."

But utter depravity is the natural understanding of Total Depravity as Calvinists define it. The doctrine of Total Depravity says we are totally (utterly) in sin from the moment we are conceived, incapable of doing anything good in the eyes of God. We cannot seek God, be reasoned with, or in any other way have anything to do with responding to God's appeals to us through His Word or the Holy Spirit's conviction.

Total Depravity to the Calvinist becomes Total Inability to humbly come to God. The historic definition of Total Depravity is a prerequisite to the Calvinist's doctrine of Unconditional Election, which teaches that God must unconditionally choose those who He elects to save without any consideration of what the man or woman has done, since they can do nothing to seek after God. Calvinists often use the Scriptures below to drive this point home:

> **Ephesians 2:1-3** *And you He made alive,* ***who were dead in trespasses and sins,*** *in which you once walked according to the course of this world, according to the prince of the power of the air, the spirit who now works in the sons of disobedience, among whom also we all once conducted ourselves in the lusts of our flesh, fulfilling the desires of the flesh and of the mind, and were by nature children of wrath, just as the others.*

> **Romans 3:9-12** *What then? Are we better than they? Not at all. For we have previously charged both Jews and Greeks that they are all under sin. As it is written: "There is none righteous, no, not one; there is none who understands; there is none who seeks after God. They have all turned aside; they have together become unprofitable; there is none who does good, no, not one."*

The quote in the Romans passage above is from Psalm 14:1-3:

> *The fool has said in his heart,* ***"There is no God."*** *They are corrupt, they have done abominable works, there is none who does good. The Lord looks down from heaven upon the children of men, to see if there are any who understand, who seek God. They have all turned aside, they have together become corrupt; there is none who does good, no, not one.*

In context, "there is none who does good" is talking about the adult rejecter of God "being dead in trespasses and sins." Death in this context is spiritual death—that is, the person's sins have now separated them from God. Despite what the Calvinists teach, this does not mean that God cannot reason with this "dead" person:

> **Isaiah 1:15-20** *"When you spread out your hands, I will hide My eyes from you; even though you make many prayers, I will not hear. Your hands are full of blood. Wash **yourselves**, make **yourselves** clean; put away the evil of your doings from before My eyes. **Cease to do evil,** learn to do good; **seek** justice, rebuke the oppressor; defend the fatherless, plead for the widow.*
>
> *"Come now, and **let us reason together,**" says the Lord, "Though your sins are like scarlet, they shall be as white as snow; though they are red like crimson, they shall be as wool. **If you are willing** and obedient, you shall eat the good of the land; but **if you refuse** and **rebel**, you shall be devoured by the sword;" for the mouth of the Lord has spoken.*

How does God reason with sinful man? Through His Word and the Holy Spirit:

> **Genesis 4:4-7** *Abel also brought of the firstborn of his flock and of their fat. And the Lord respected Abel and his offering, but He did not respect Cain and his offering. And Cain was very angry, and his countenance fell. So the Lord said to Cain, "Why are you angry? And why has your countenance fallen? If **you** do well, will you not be accepted? And if **you** do not do well, sin lies at the door. And its desire is for you, **but you should rule over it."***

God Himself was reasoning with Cain, exhorting him to do what God had commanded and warning him of the consequences if he didn't.

> **John 16:8** *And when He has come, He will convict the world of sin, and of righteousness, and of judgment: of sin, because they do not believe in Me; of righteousness, because I go to My Father and you see Me no more; of judgment, because the ruler of this world is judged.*

The Holy Spirit is sent to convict the world of sin and warn of judgment. The Calvinist teaching on Total Depravity is contrary to God's Word in that it teaches that man—from conception until death, unless unconditionally elected by God—is **utterly dead** and therefore *utterly unable* to receive instruction, be reasoned with, come under conviction, or repent so as to avoid judgment.

> R.C. Sproul – "You might think of an archfiend of history such as Adolf Hitler and say there was absolutely no **redeeming virtue** in the man, but I suspect that he had some affection for his mother. As wicked as Hitler was, we can still conceive of ways in which he could have been even more wicked than he actually was. So the idea of total in Total Depravity doesn't mean that all human beings are as wicked as they can possibly be. It means that the fall was so serious that it affects **the whole person.**"

This statement is self-contradictory. If the whole person is affected, then what part of Hitler was nice to his mother? If Hitler had affection for his mother, did he have "redeeming value?" Calvinist dogma states that it is impossible for a "dead in trespasses and sins" person to do anything good or have any "redeeming value."

How did Hitler come to have affection for his mother rather than send her to a gas chamber? If Hitler was somehow able to have affection for his mother, how could it be impossible for him to come to have affection for God?

> R.C. Sproul – "It [fallenness] affects our minds and our thinking; we still have the capacity to think, but the Bible says the mind has become darkened and weakened. The will of man is no longer in its pristine state of moral power. The will, according to the New Testament, is now in bondage. We are enslaved to the evil impulses and desires of our

> hearts. The body, the mind, the will, the spirit—indeed, the whole person—have been infected by the power of sin. I like to replace the term **Total Depravity** with my favorite designation, which is **radical corruption**."

For 400 years (since Synod of Dort in 1619), Calvinists have been using "Total Depravity" or "Depravity, Native and Total." Now Sproul suggests a change to "Radical Corruption."

> R.C. Sproul – "Ironically, the word *radical* has its roots in the Latin word for "root," which is *radix*, and it can be translated root or *core*. The term radical has to do with something that permeates to the core of a thing. It's not something that is tangential or superficial, lying on the surface."

Here, Sproul employs etymological gymnastics to introduce concepts that have nothing to do with the topic at hand. So "Total Depravity" becomes "Radical Corruption" which is then changed to "Core Depravity," seeming to imply the outside can be "not depraved" because "Total Depravity" cannot mean "utter" depravity because Hitler had affection for his mother. Thus the "whole person" is not depraved, contradicting what Sproul said earlier.

If he were alive, I would want to hear Dr. Sproul explain all of this in light of David's life when he was a single-cell baby in the womb of his mother. How did his core of corruption differ from his "tangential or superficial" being? What part of baby David had redeeming value and thus kept him from being Totally/Utterly Depraved?

> R.C. Sproul – "The Reformed view is that the effects of the fall extend or penetrate to the core of our being. Even the English word core actually comes from the Latin word **cor**, which means "heart." That is, our sin is something that

> comes from our hearts. In biblical terms, that means it's from the core or very center of our existence."

Yes, there is no dispute that the heart of fallen man is rebellious against God and thus wicked, but Jeremiah cannot possibly be inspired by God to be addressing children in the womb:

> **Jeremiah 17:9,10** *The heart is deceitful above all things, and desperately wicked; who can know it? I, the Lord, search the heart, I test the mind, even to give every man according to his ways, according to the fruit of his doings.*

Also notice that God does not call the fallen heart of man "totally depraved." The Scripture says He [God] searches the heart and tests the mind in order to give every man according to his ways and according to the fruit of his doing. God acknowledges that man is able to do good and, according to the Scriptures, even to seek God (Hebrews 11:6), repent (Jeremiah 25:5, Matthew 4:17, Acts 17:30 and 26:20), receive God's forgiveness after believing (Acts 13:38,39, 26:17,18, Col 1:15-18), and receive a new heart (Jeremiah 31:33,34, Hebrews 10:16,17).

> R.C. Sproul – "So what is required for us to be conformed to the image of Christ is not simply some small adjustments or behavioral modifications, but nothing less than renovation from the inside. We need to be regenerated, to be made over again, to be quickened by the power of the Spirit. The only way in which a person can escape this radical situation is by the Holy Spirit's changing the core, the heart."

Calvinists believe this "renovation" of the heart/core happens only when God forces it by Unconditional Election using Irresistible Grace, as explained briefly in the Summary section. These dogmas teach that a totally depraved person must be regenerated (born again) before he/she can believe and be saved.

But Jesus tells Nicodemus in John Chapter 3 that *he* must be born again. If Calvinists are right, why would Jesus tell Nicodemus that he must be born again if doing so is impossible for Nicodemus since he is totally depraved and unable to seek or respond to God's offer of salvation? If Sproul is right, then why didn't Jesus just level with Nicodemus and tell him whether he was elected to be saved or destined to be damned?

If Nicodemus were one of the very few that God had decided to unconditionally elect, why didn't Jesus explain to Nicodemus when God was going to flip Nicodemus' switch thus allowing him to be one of the beneficiaries of Jesus' limited atonement, then put the irresistible grace of God at the nose of Nicodemus who is unable to resist God's grace and at that moment is regenerated (born again) allowing Nicodemus to then believe and become saved?

For those unfamiliar with these other points of Calvinism (Unconditional Election, Limited Atonement, and Irresistible Grace), I cover them in more detail later. You can also familiarize yourself with the Calvinist perspective by going to the late R.C. Sproul's website. But beware, his twisting of Scripture and wisdom-of-man arguments are just as contrary to the true loving nature of the God of the Bible as are his arguments for Original Sin and Total Depravity, which are covered here.

If Nicodemus was destined to be part of the majority who God in His sovereignty destined to go to the Lake of Fire, why didn't Jesus just tell Nicodemus his future? Why didn't Jesus tell him to go back to the Pharisee crowd and stop seeking Jesus, because a future theologian will say that he is incapable of doing so? Could it be because Jesus was not a Calvinist, that He reasoned with Nicodemus and encouraged him to be born again because Jesus knew that Nicodemus could do so by humbling himself, believing, and calling upon the name of the Lord?

Why do We Die Physically?

> R.C. Sproul – "The fallenness that captures and grips our human nature affects our bodies; that's why we become ill and die."

This statement is unbiblical. The Bible actually teaches that we become ill and die because we no longer have access to the Tree of Life, another consequence of the Fall.

> **Genesis 3:22-24** *Then the Lord God said, "Behold, the man has become like one of Us, to know good and evil. And now,* **lest he put out his hand and take also of the tree of life, and eat, and live forever**" — *therefore the Lord God sent him out of the garden of Eden to till the ground from which he was taken. So He drove out the man; and He placed cherubim at the east of the garden of Eden, and a flaming sword which turned every way, to guard the way to the tree of life.*

Consistent Calvinists teach that babies are considered by God to be sinners while they are in the womb because the *"wages of sin is death"* (Romans 6:23) and some babies die before birth. I have even heard a popular Calvinist pastor teach his congregation about his difficulty in trying to comfort parents who have lost their baby, because he and the parents are unable to know that their child is in heaven. He taught that God is sovereign and only He knows whether that particular child was unconditionally elected to go to heaven instead of hell.

However, Romans 6:23 refers to *spiritual* death, not *physical* death. God Himself makes this clear when He said to Adam, *"On the day that you eat of it* [the fruit of the tree of the knowledge of good and evil], *you shall surely die* (Genesis 2:17). We know that Adam and Eve did not *physically* die on the day they ate of the fruit, but they *did* die *spiritually* when they lost their perfect relationship with God.

From the passage in Genesis 3, Adam and Eve would have lived forever in their fallen nature if they had been allowed continued access to the Tree of Life.

One can even argue that Jesus took our sins upon Himself at the moment He cried out, "My God, My God, why have You forsaken me?" (Matthew 27:46). It appears that it was at this moment Jesus lost His fellowship with the Father, and thus died "spiritually." Soon after, Jesus experienced physical death in fulfillment of Daniel's prophecy in Chapter 9, verse 26, where it says that the Messiah would be "cut off":

> **Daniel 9:26** *And after the sixty-two weeks Messiah shall be cut off, but not for Himself;*

The Hebrew word for "cut off" is *karath* (kaw-rath'). According to Vines Expository Dictionary, one of the best-known uses of this verb is "to **make**" a covenant. The process by which God **made** a covenant with Abraham and the Jews is called "*cutting* a covenant."

> **Genesis 15:17,18** *And it came to pass, when the sun went down and it was dark, that behold, there appeared a smoking oven and a burning torch that passed between those pieces [of the animal sacrifices]. On the same day the Lord* **made** *[Hebrew karath] a covenant with Abram, saying: "To your descendants I have given this land, from the river of Egypt to the great river, the River Euphrates —*

> **Exodus 24:8** *And Moses took the* **blood**, *sprinkled it on the people, and said, "This is the blood of the covenant which the Lord has* **made** *[Hebrew karath] with you according to all these words."*

Daniel 9:26 was prophesying that the Messiah/Jesus would be sacrificially killed by shedding His blood thus establishing the New Covenant that God promised in Jeremiah 31 and Matthew 26:28, which was fulfilled in Jesus' sacrifice as noted in Hebrews, Chapters 8-9, a portion highlighted here:

Hebrews 9:13-15 *For if the blood of bulls and goats and the ashes of a heifer, sprinkling the unclean, sanctifies for the purifying of the flesh, how much more shall the blood of Christ, who through the eternal Spirit offered Himself without spot to God, cleanse your conscience from dead works to serve the living God? And for this reason He is the **Mediator of the new covenant**, by means of death, for the redemption of the transgressions under the first covenant, that those who are called may receive the promise of the eternal inheritance.*

According to the Received Text (the Greek *Textus Receptus* of the New Testament which was used by the translators of the King James and New King James versions of the Bible), we see from John 3:13 that before God forsook Jesus on the cross (spiritual death), Jesus had perfect and complete union with the Father to the extent that while He was on earth, He was also in heaven:

John 3:13 *No one has ascended to heaven but He who came down from heaven, that is, the Son of Man **who is in heaven**.*

The unbiblical belief that "*the wages of sin is death*" means *physical* death as well as spiritual death—and is thus "proof" that a person's sin originates in the womb because some babies die—can lead to other errors. For example, Scripture clearly teaches that we are saved by Jesus' atoning blood. But prominent Calvinist and pastor, John MacArthur, teaches that we are not saved by Jesus' blood, but by His physical death, because "*the wages of sin is death.*" See MacArthur's teaching, "Are We Saved by Jesus Physical Blood?" at *youtu.be/rE6JPy75BmE*.

In the video linked above, Pastor MacArthur teaches,

"If Jesus had just bled, nobody would be saved. **The wages of sin is not bleeding; the wages of sin is death.** People must understand: it's not the bleeding of Jesus, and it's not the blood of Jesus. To speak of the "blood of the cross"

> ... is to simply speak of the efficacious, substitutionary sacrificial death of Christ. Do I think he had to ... actually bleed? Not to save us, but to fulfill the Old Testament picture. Somebody suggested that I might have thought he could be bludgeoned to death. **Well, I suppose if God had decided that's the way he had to die, that would be fine,** but the pattern and the picture of the shedding of blood was in the whole Old Testament sacrificial system. And as the fulfillment of the final lamb, [Jesus] fit that model and that pattern. But we are not saved by his blood.
>
> There's this weird theology that floats around, that people have turned the blood into a fetish. ... There's nothing magic in Jesus' blood ... or his saliva, or any other part of the fluids of the human body. ... We're talking about his death, and **blood is a euphemistic way to refer to his death,** particularly when you realize the bloodshed that occurred [at Calvary]. ... We're not saved by his bleeding, or his blood as a fluid, but by his death."

But the Bible says:

> **Leviticus 17:10,11** *'And whatever man of the house of Israel, or of the strangers who dwell among you, who eats any blood, I will set My face against that person who eats blood, and will cut him off from among his people. For the life of the flesh is in the blood, and I have given it to you upon the altar to make* **atonement for your souls;** *for* **it is the blood that makes atonement for the soul.'**
>
> **Hebrews 9:12** *Not with the blood of goats and calves, but* **with His own blood He entered the Most Holy Place once for all,** *having obtained eternal redemption.*
>
> **Hebrews 9:22** *And according to the law almost all things are* **purified with blood,** *and* **without shedding of blood there is no remission.**

1 Peter 1:1,2; 17-19 *Peter, an apostle of Jesus Christ, To the pilgrims of the Dispersion in Pontus, Galatia, Cappadocia, Asia, and Bithynia, elect according to the foreknowledge of God the Father, in sanctification of the Spirit, for obedience and* **sprinkling of the blood of Jesus Christ:** *Grace to you and peace be multiplied. ---- And if you call on the Father, who without partiality judges according to each one's work, conduct yourselves throughout the time of your stay here in fear; knowing that you were not redeemed with corruptible things, like silver or gold, from your aimless conduct received by tradition from your fathers,* **but with the precious blood of Christ,** *as of a lamb without blemish and without spot.*

(Also see Matthew 26:28, Luke 22:20, Acts 20:28, Romans 3:25, Romans 5:9, Ephesians 2:13, Colossians 1:14, Colossians 1:20, Revelation 1:5, Revelation 7:14, Hebrews 10:29.)

The Scarlet Thread

The "scarlet thread" throughout the Old Testament pointed to the day Jesus would shed His blood on our behalf, providing salvation to all those who believe that His blood sacrifice somehow mysteriously was taken to the mercy seat in heaven on our behalf (Hebrews 9:12). His shed blood spiritually applied to our hearts when we receive His salvation by faith is what allows spiritual death to pass over the Christian in the same way the shed blood of the lamb on the doorpost of the house protected the first born Jews inside during the first Passover (Exodus 12).

Jesus replaced all the animal sacrifices under the Old Covenant (see book of Hebrews). But before He did so, the Priests would take the *blood* of the animal sacrifices into the Tabernacle/Temple and then sprinkle the *blood* at the veil, on the altar of incense, and/or at the brazen altar of sacrifice. They did not take the dead body of the sacrificial animal into the Tabernacle/Temple and wave it around saying, "Here God, this is the strangled dead bull, goat, ram, lamb, pigeon as an offering for sin, etc."

For Pastor John MacArthur to suggest that *"If God had decided that's the way [bludgeoning to death] He [Jesus] had to die, that would be fine"* is an egregious example of elevating the teachings of Calvin above the inspired Word of God.

Why is this difference in emphasis so important? *Because if physical death is the proof of sinfulness, then babies are sinful at conception*—and Augustine and the Reformers are correct in their belief that Total Depravity is our initial human condition upon coming into this world.

But if spiritual death, not physical death, is what is meant by *"the wages of sin is death"*—and the Bible makes it clear that it is—then babies who die before or after birth are not doing so because they are sinners in the eyes of God. Thus, they are *not* Totally Depraved as Calvinists teach, and are therefore all in heaven. *It is not until the person sins against God that they become a sinner.* At that moment they are "spiritually dead" —meaning separated from God and destined for judgment unless they call upon the name of the Lord to be saved.

> PASTOR KEVIN LEA — Tweet this: *"You become a sinner in the eyes of God when you have sinned against God."*

Reasoning from the Scriptures, therefore, we see that the physical death of babies does not prove that they are sinners; it simply shows that all of creation was corrupted at the fall of man. This is why true believers join with the creation in groaning together as we wait for the quickly approaching day our Lord Jesus returns to restore all things and to wipe away our tears (Romans 8:18-23, Revelation 21:4).

Scripture Refutes the Unbiblical Doctrine of Total Depravity

The following few verses from the Old and New Testaments refute the Calvinist doctrine of Total Depravity. Examples could be multiplied:

Old Testament Verses

(All verses are from the NKJV)

> **Genesis 4:4-7** *Abel also brought of the firstborn of his flock and of their fat. And the Lord respected Abel and his offering, but He did not respect Cain and his offering. And Cain was very angry, and his countenance fell. So the Lord said to Cain, "Why are you angry? And why has your countenance fallen? If you do well, will you not be accepted? And if you do not do well, sin lies at the door. And its desire is for you,* **but you should rule over it.**"

How can Cain rule over sin if he is Totally Depraved?

> **Deuteronomy 4:29** *"But from there you will seek the LORD your God, and you will find Him if you seek Him with all your heart and with all your soul."*

> **Psalm 9:10** *And those who know your name will put their trust in you; for you, Lord, have not forsaken those who seek you.*

> **Psalm 34:2-4** *My soul shall make its boast in the LORD; the humble shall hear of it and be glad. Oh, magnify the LORD with me, and let us exalt His name together. I sought the LORD, and He heard me, and delivered me from all my fears.*

> **Proverbs 8:17** *I love those who love me, and those who seek me diligently will find me.*

> **Isaiah 45:19** *I have not spoken in secret, in a dark place of the earth; I did not say to the seed of Jacob, 'Seek Me in vain'; I, the LORD, speak righteousness, I declare things that are right.*

How can the Jews seek the Lord if they are Totally Depraved?

> **Deuteronomy 30:1** *"I call heaven and earth as witnesses today against you, that I have set before you life and death, blessing and cursing; therefore choose life, that both you and your descendants may live;*

How can the Jews *choose* life or death if they are Totally Depraved? Also, according to Calvin, it is God who has already *determined* those whom He damns and those whom He saves. So why is God inspiring Moses to exhort all the people to *choose* life if it is not possible for most to do so?

> **Ezekiel 33:11** *"Say to them: 'As I live,' says the Lord GOD, 'I have no pleasure in the death of the wicked, but that the wicked turn from his way and live. Turn, turn from your evil ways! For why should you die, O house of Israel?'*

How can the wicked turn from his evil ways if he/she is Totally Depraved and unable to do so?

New Testament Verses

(All verses are from the NKJV)

> **Matthew 8:10** *When Jesus heard it, He marveled, and said to those who followed, "Assuredly, I say to you, I have not found such great faith, not even in Israel!*

Matthew 15:28 *Then Jesus answered and said to her, "O woman, great is your faith! Let it be to you as you desire." And her daughter was healed from that very hour.*

Why does Jesus commend the Roman centurion (Matthew 8:10) and the Gentile woman from Tyre and Sidon (Matthew 15:28) for their faith if a Totally Depraved person cannot have faith? In addition, contrary to the Greek, some Calvinists believe that it is Faith, not Grace, that is the gift of Ephesians 2:8:

Ephesians 2:8,9 *"For by grace you have been saved through faith, and that not of yourselves; it is the gift of God, not of works, lest anyone should boast.*

The Greek understanding of the neuter/feminine pronouns in this passage indicates that grace, not faith, is the gift of God. The inspired Scriptures confirm this in Romans 10:17 which proclaims, *"So then faith comes by hearing, and hearing by the word of God."*

Even common sense informs us that the presenter of a gift does not commend the receiver of that gift for *already having* the gift that the presenter gave them! Neither does Jesus commend people for their faith unless it was "their" faith that came alive when they believed in the Word of God. When a person believes with biblical faith, then God gifts them with His grace and everlasting life.

Luke 15:7, 10 *"I say to you that likewise there will be more joy in heaven over one sinner who repents than over ninety-nine just persons who need no repentance. "Likewise, I say to you, there is joy in the presence of the angels of God over one sinner who repents."*

Why does Jesus commend those who repent if they can't do so according to Total Depravity?

Acts 17:27 *"so that they should seek the Lord, in the hope that they might grope for Him and find Him, though He is not far from each one of us;*

Again, why does Jesus inspire Paul to exhort unbelievers to seek the Lord if they are Totally Depraved? How is God not "far from each one of us" if God has chosen that most people are to be damned to hell and are thus very far from Him?

I exhort the reader who has been trapped in the Calvinist web to put all of your Calvinist books down and just read God's Word from Genesis to Revelation. If you do, you will note the thousands of times the inspired writers reveal a loving God Who is reaching out to sinful mankind, exhorting *"whosoever will"* to turn to Him.

Summary

Total Depravity

The Calvinist doctrines of Original Sin and associated Total Depravity are based upon modern paraphrases of a *single* Scripture verse—Psalm 51:5. These paraphrase versions are not word-for-word translations, and they are worded by modern translators to support the Calvinist premise that we are sinners from the moment of conception in the womb.

Thus, it can be clearly seen that Total Depravity is the essential foundation of TULIP—without which "ULI" is not only completely unnecessary, but entirely untenable. The following is a brief reasoning for saying this.

Unconditional Election

A Calvinist friend of mine took exception to my assertion that if "T," the Calvinist doctrine of Total Depravity, crumbles, so does "ULI." He challenged me to address "U," the Calvinist doctrine of Unconditional Election, which I do so here.

First, it is irrefutable from Scripture that God *does* elect those who are saved. The real debate is not about election; it is about whether God's election is *conditional* or *unconditional*.

Second, if the Calvinist doctrine of Total Depravity is true, then yes, God's election of those He capriciously chooses to save must be unconditional, without any regard to their spiritual "condition." How could it be otherwise?

However, the Calvinist doctrine of Unconditional Election fails if people can:

- Respond in humility to the preaching of creation (Romans 1, 2:12-16)

- Respond in humility to the conviction of the Holy Spirit (John 16:7,8)

- Humble themselves and repent when awareness of their own sin moves them to call upon the name of the Lord for mercy (Luke 10:21,22; Luke 18:13,14) or

- Listen when an ambassador of Jesus pleads with them and respond in faith by calling upon the name of the Lord (Acts 16:30-34, Romans 10:8-17, 2 Cor 5:18-21).

Since the Scriptures cited above (and many more) prove that *all* the above are true, we see that God opens the spiritual eyes and saves (elects) those who humble themselves before Him in repentance and faith. Conversely, God resists the proud, electing them to damnation. Thus, Scripture clearly teaches *conditional*, not *unconditional*, election to salvation.

Further, the following words from Jesus Himself, along with the prior Scripture-based refutation of Original Sin and Total Depravity, demolishes the Calvinist doctrine of Unconditional Election:

> **Luke 10:21,22** *In that hour Jesus rejoiced in the Spirit and said, "I thank You, Father, Lord of heaven and earth, that You have* **hidden these things from the wise and prudent** *[the proud] and* **revealed them to babes** *[the humble]. Even so, Father, for so it seemed good in Your sight. All things have been delivered to Me by My Father, and no one knows who the Son is except the Father, and who the Father is except the Son, and the one to whom the Son wills to reveal Him"* [the humble "babes" above].

Jesus clarifies conditional election further in the parable of the wedding feast in Matthew 22:1-14. The **condition** for being allowed to attend the wedding feast is proper wedding garments, interpreted as white robes of righteousness given to those who have faith in Jesus (Revelation 6:11). When a man is found to be without proper attire, he is cast out. Jesus concludes the parable with, *"Many are called, few are chosen."* As the parable makes clear, the man was called to attend the wedding feast, but he was not chosen to stay because he came without receiving God's gift of imputed righteousness.

By way of analogy, consider a dog whistle. When blown, dogs hear it, but humans cannot because our ears cannot detect the high frequency of the sound waves produced by the whistle.

God's invitation of salvation has gone out to the entire world (*many are called*):

> **Psalm 19:1-5** *The heavens declare the glory of God; and the firmament shows His handiwork. Day unto day utters speech, and night unto night reveals knowledge. There is no speech nor language where their voice is not heard. Their line has gone out through all the earth, and their words to the end of the world. In them He has set a tabernacle for the sun, which is like a bridegroom coming out of his chamber, and rejoices like a strong man to run its race.*

But the ears of a prideful person are not "tuned" to hear God's call and respond to His gospel (*hidden these things from the wise and prudent*, Luke 10:21). However, when people choose to become humble, God opens their ears to hear and they become "chosen" as Jesus reveals Himself to them.

However, for those like my friend, who need additional proof that salvation is conditional, not unconditional, I will present a rebuttal to R.C. Sproul's use of Romans 9 as a proof text of Unconditional Election and evaluate other statements he makes at:

https://www.ligonier.org/blog/tulip-and-reformed-theology-unconditional-election/, "TULIP and Reformed Theology: Unconditional Election."

Please note that Sproul's statements are all tied to the assumption that Total Depravity is true.

> R.C. Sproul – "The Reformed [Calvinist] view of **election**, known as Unconditional Election, means that God does not foresee an action or condition on our part that induces Him to save us. **Rather, election rests on God's sovereign decision to save whomever He is pleased to save. . . ."**

> R.C. Sproul – "In the book of Romans, we find a discussion of this difficult concept. Romans 9:10–13 reads: *"And not only so, but also when Rebekah had conceived children by one man, our forefather Isaac, though they were not yet born and had done nothing either good or bad—in order that God's purpose of **election** might continue, not because of works but because of him who calls—she was told, 'The older will serve the younger.' As it is written, 'Jacob I loved, but Esau I hated.'"* Here the Apostle Paul is giving his exposition of the doctrine of election."

The foremost rule of biblical hermeneutics is that context is critical and primary for an accurate interpretation of Scripture. This is because, without regard for context, anyone can "prove" anything from Scripture. Calvinists often pick out verses about God's choosing (electing) of and/or His mercy towards people as "proof" of Unconditional Election **to salvation**, when the context reveals that something completely different is being discussed.

For example, in the Romans passage above, *God is **not** saying that Jacob would be eternally saved and Esau would be eternally damned.* He is saying that Jacob would receive the *birthright* passed from Abraham, Isaac, and now to Jacob. The birthright was the promise from God to Abraham (Genesis 12:2, 3, 7) that a great nation would come through him; that He would bless those who bless him (Abraham, Isaac, Jacob, the Jews) and curse those who cursed him; that through his descendants, all the nations would be blessed (a prophecy that the Messiah would now come through Jacob and not Esau); and that Jacob's descendants, the Jews, would inherit the land.

A careful reading of Romans Chapters 9 through 11 shows that Paul is speaking of the role the Jews will play as God's chosen people throughout history – the people group God chose to reveal Himself to all the nations of the world. When Romans 9:11 says, *"that the purpose of **election** might continue, not because of works but because of Him who calls,"* it is telling us that God decided to grant the birthright, the Abrahamic Covenant, to the younger twin (Jacob), even though the human rule would automatically grant the birthright to the elder (Esau).

> R.C. Sproul – "He [Paul] deals with it significantly in Romans 8, but here he illustrates his teaching of the doctrine of election by going back into the past of the Jewish people and looking at the circumstances surrounding the birth of twins—Jacob and Esau. In the ancient world, it was customary for the firstborn son to receive the inheritance or the patriarchal blessing. However, in the case of these twins, God reversed the process and gave the blessing not to the elder but to the younger. The point that the Apostle labors here is that God not only makes this decision prior to the twins' births, He does it without a view to anything they would do, either good or evil, so that the purposes of God might stand. Therefore, **our salvation** does not rest on us; it rests solely on the gracious, sovereign decision of God."

Observe in the quote above how R.C. Sproul switches the subject from election of the *birthright*—which is the context—to election to *personal salvation*.

> R.C. Sproul – "The point that the Apostle labors here is that God not only makes this decision prior to the twins' births, He does it **without a view** to anything they would do, either good or evil, so that the purposes of God might stand."

Note that the *Scripture* does *not* say that God made the determination "without a view." Rather, it is R.C. Sproul who asserts this. Romans 9:12, which quotes Genesis 25:23, simply states that God prophetically told the twins' mother that the older would serve the younger before the two children were even born and able to do good or bad. *This prophecy had **nothing to do with their spiritual salvation** and therefore has nothing to do with the Calvinist Unconditional Election (to salvation).*

God is omniscient – He is all-knowing and stands outside of time. Did the all-knowing God foresee that Esau would despise his birthright and sell it to Jacob, who cherished the birthright of the father? Most certainly, yes. It fits the character and purpose of God in glorifying Himself to give the blessing of the birthright to the one who wanted it instead of one who despised it.

God's prophecy to Rebekah is analogous to His prophecy to Isaiah that there would be a King named Cyrus who would allow the Jews to return to Israel and rebuild the temple. God did so more than one hundred years before Cyrus was born (before he had done either good or bad) (Isaiah 44:26-28). God's election of Cyrus to allow the Jews to return to Israel and build the temple also had nothing to do with whether Cyrus was spiritually saved or not.

But RC Sproul **does** equate the Genesis passage pertaining to Jacob and Esau to God's election for salvation. Calvinists believe that God elects who is going to be spiritually saved and who is going to be damned to the Lake of Fire before they are born *"that the purpose of God according to election might stand, not of works but of Him who calls."* To support this view, they twist the Scripture.

We see again how critical the rule of context is when evaluating Sproul's earlier comment quoting Romans 9:10-13. Verse 13 says, *"As it is written, 'Jacob I loved, but Esau I hated."* By including this verse without comment, Sproul leaves the unschooled reader to conclude that God loved baby Jacob in the womb and hated baby Esau in the womb. But let's look carefully at the text, considering the context, to see that this is *not* what this passage is saying.

> **Romans 9:10-12** *"And not only so, but also when Rebekah had conceived children by one man, our forefather Isaac, though they were not yet born and had done nothing either good or bad—in order that God's purpose of election might continue, not because of works but because of him who calls—she was told, 'The older will serve the younger.'"*
>
> **Romans 9:13** *"As it is written,* **'Jacob I loved, but Esau I hated.'"**

In Romans 9:10-12 above, Paul is quoting Genesis 25:23. In verse 13, Paul is quoting Malachi 1:2-5, written about 1400 years after Jacob and Esau were born:

> **Malachi 1:2-5** *"I have loved you," says the Lord. "Yet you say, 'In what way have You loved us?'" "Was not Esau Jacob's brother?" says the Lord. "Yet Jacob I have loved; but Esau I have hated and laid waste his mountains and his heritage for the jackals of the wilderness." Even though Edom has said, "We have been impoverished, but we will return and build the desolate places," thus says the Lord of hosts: "They may build, but I will throw down; they shall be called the territory of wickedness, and the people against whom the Lord will have indignation forever. Your eyes*

shall see, and you shall say, 'The Lord is magnified beyond the border of Israel."

Looking at the Malachi quote in context, we see that God calls the Nation of Israel "Jacob" (as He does in many other places in Scripture) and He refers to the nation of Edom as "Esau," its founder.

With this context in mind, we see that Paul in Romans 9:13 is simply affirming that even though God has set the Jews apart as a witness people for a time because they rejected Jesus as their Messiah, He *will* keep His covenant promises to Jacob (Israel), and they *will* be preserved as a witness people until the Second Coming of Jesus. History has documented the fulfillment of this promise. The Jews were dispersed from their land twice and restored twice:

First, they were carried away into captivity by the Babylonians in 586 B.C. and allowed to return by the decree of Cyrus the Mede in 534 B.C. The nation was destroyed the second time by the Romans in A.D. 70, followed by nearly 1900 years of dispersion. On November 29, 1947, the United Nations passed a resolution to partition Palestine, resulting in the restoration of Israel to statehood on May 14, 1948.

In contrast, God made no such promises to the descendants of Esau who hated their Jewish relatives, repeatedly fought against them, and rejoiced at their conquest by Babylon in 586 B.C. As a result, God "hated Esau" in comparison to His covenant love for Jacob. That is, He allowed the Edomites to be destroyed, never to be restored. Again, history documents the fulfillment of this prophecy. The nation of Edom was conquered several times over the years and was completely destroyed as a sovereign nation by the time of Christ.

Like his doctrine of Total Depravity, which relies *solely* on Psalm 51:5, Sproul bases the second major doctrine of Calvinism, Unconditional Election, on a single section of Scripture, Romans 9:10-16, which he takes out of context. Sproul's other arguments in support of Unconditional Election are based on his own (human) reasoning:

> R.C. Sproul [repeated here for clarity] – "The point that the Apostle labors here is that God not only makes this decision prior to the twins' births, He does it **without a view** to anything they would do, either good or evil, so that the purposes of God might stand."

> R.C. Sproul – "Therefore, **our salvation** does not rest on us; it rests solely on the gracious, sovereign decision of God."

> "Tweet this – GOD DOES NOT FORESEE AN ACTION OR CONDITION ON OUR PART THAT INDUCES HIM TO SAVE US. —R.C. SPROUL"

> R.C. Sproul – "This doesn't mean that God will save people whether they come to faith or not. There are conditions that God decrees for salvation, not the least of which is putting one's personal trust in Christ."

One of my Calvinist friends has admitted more than once during our discussions that Calvinist writings are often self-contradictory, and this is a prime example. Sproul's statement above completely contradicts the earlier arguments at his web posting. How can he defend *Unconditional* Election to salvation by saying that there *are* conditions for salvation? One would think it would be impossible to even try, but try he does:

> R.C. Sproul – "However, that is a condition for justification, and the doctrine of election is something else. When we're talking about Unconditional Election, we're talking in a very narrow confine of the doctrine of election itself."

If this sounds confusing, it's because it is. But let's try to follow this rabbit trail. Calvinists believe that God elects to salvation one person over another, without any consideration for what that person thinks or does pertaining to believing in God. Then God converts the elected person using irresistible grace, which is God's way of forcing open their eyes to God. Now that the person has been forced to have his eyes opened by God's irresistible grace, the person must respond by putting their trust in God to receive justification / salvation.

It is interesting that Calvinists believe that a person cannot have free will to seek God, but they have the condition (free will) to believe. So, if Calvinists say that God can give man free will after they are elected but before being saved, why cannot God elect to give man free will from birth, as the Bible clearly teaches but Calvinists deny?

Calvinists often say, "You must be born again before you can be saved." Sproul is saying that man can do nothing until he is converted by the sovereign Unconditional Election of God, but then there is a condition that person must meet for them to be justified, "*not the least of which is putting one's personal trust in Christ.*" So, man does not and cannot have free will until and unless God makes His grace irresistible to them, but then they *do* have free will to either believe in Him or not. (The unbiblical concept of "Irresistible Grace" is the "I," the fourth major tenet of Calvinism.)

To help you wrap your head around this twisted human logic, consider this analogy:

A man is conceived in the womb with a hatred for ice cream. From birth it is impossible for him to seek after, taste, or hear about the delight of tasting ice cream from anyone who loves ice cream. This person is cursed to forever hate ice cream (and go to hell), unless God randomly elects him to be one of the few that is allowed to not only like, but rather crave, ice cream to the point that it is impossible for him to resist it.

Once randomly elected, God then opens his senses to see and smell chocolate ice cream (pick your flavor if you don't like chocolate). A bowl of chocolate ice cream sits before him. The sight and smell produce a dopamine rush that sweeps over him as with a meth addict given a loaded syringe, knowing another high is only moments away. He can't wait to take a spoon full of the irresistible delicacy that he never knew existed before.

BUT WAIT, there is a CONDITION – he cannot have the ice cream unless, by his free will, he chooses to pick up the spoon and put some in his mouth (a "condition" implies the person can refuse to believe after Unconditional Election and irresistible grace). Can the person refuse to pick up the spoon and eat? Not according to the Calvinist doctrine of irresistible grace. Therefore, there is no "condition" (ability to believe or not believe) unless irresistible grace is another unbiblical Calvinist fabrication (which it is).

When we see Calvinist statements like, "there is a condition that a person must meet for them to be justified," we must understand that they are merely Band-Aids, human stopgaps, to make their soteriology (doctrine of salvation) appear sound. The Scriptures are very clear that man *believes* onto *salvation*. Calvinists do not want to say that God *makes* them believe so they come up with a twisted human argument that God Unconditionally Elects, uses Irresistible Grace to force them to be born again, and then allows them to believe so they can be saved. But either Irresistible Grace is not truly irresistible, or man under Calvinism cannot himself choose to believe, he must be forced to do so.

This convoluted doctrine presents another problem for Calvinists. As we saw earlier, consistent Calvinists believe that unelected babies go to hell, while elected babies go to heaven. But how does an unconditionally elected baby become born again and then believe unto salvation? The steps to Calvinist salvation include God's irresistible grace and then being presented with the condition that they must now, "put their personal trust in Christ" in order to be saved, something that is impossible for infants to do. Thus, the supposed elected baby cannot be saved, according to this doctrine. Therefore, according to Calvinist dogma, all babies and children who are too young to put their personal trust in Christ are destined to be sent to the lake of fire when they die.

> R.C. Sproul – "So, then, **on what basis** does God elect to save certain people? Is it on the basis of some foreseen reaction, response, or activity of the elect? Many people who have a doctrine of election or predestination look at it this way. They believe that in eternity past God looked down through the corridors of time and He knew in advance who would say yes to the offer of the gospel and who would say no. On the basis of this prior knowledge of those who will meet the condition for salvation—that is, expressing faith or belief in Christ—He elects to save them. This is **conditional** election, which means that God distributes His electing grace on the basis of some foreseen **condition** that human beings meet themselves."

As stated above, using multiple Scriptures from Jesus and the Apostles, conditional election was the historic view of salvation until Augustine and Calvin.

> R.C. Sproul – "**Unconditional election** is another term that I think can be a bit misleading, so I prefer to use the term **sovereign election**. If God chooses sovereignly to bestow His grace on some sinners and withhold His grace from other sinners, is there any violation of justice in this?"

Sproul *again* deviates from standard TULIP wording—which should lead discerning readers to ask, "Why?"

"Unconditional" election implies that God capriciously (impulsive, unpredictable, determined by chance, impulse or whim) elects a few to be saved and damns the rest to hell, because He doesn't want to save them. "Sovereign" election seems nicer. (How can anyone deny that God is sovereign?)

However, the God of the Bible, while sovereign, is *not* capricious. The Bible is clear that God sovereignly elects those who desire to receive His grace. It is the humble who call upon the name of the Lord to be saved. Those who *do not* (the proud) *will not*. God has made His conditional, sovereign election perfectly clear from Genesis to Revelation. If God's sovereign election is not *unconditional* nor *capricious*, then TULI falls, as it should.

Early in my ministry as a pastor, a young man attending our church, someone who embraced Calvinism, rebuked me after a service in which I had taught on the sovereignty of God without mentioning Unconditional Election. He said, "I know you believe in Unconditional Election, but you just don't want to teach it to the congregants because you want to make God look good." My response to him was that, "I don't have to 'make God look good,' because He *is* good, and that is why I don't teach Calvinist doctrine."

> R.C. Sproul – "Do those who do not receive this gift receive something they do not deserve? Of course not. If God allows

> these sinners to perish, is He treating them unjustly? Of course not."

However, any god that would unconditionally elect only a few to salvation and most to damnation is not a loving God. But the God of the Bible has clearly revealed Himself as a God of love (John 3:16, 1 John 4:8, 19 and many more). The capricious, unconditionally-electing, Calvinist god is not the same as the loving God of the Bible who elects to save all those who humbly believe in Him.

> R.C. Sproul – "One group receives grace; the other receives justice. No one receives injustice. Paul anticipates this protest: "Is there injustice on God's part?" (Romans 9:14a). He answers it with the most emphatic response he can muster. I prefer the translation, "God forbid" (v. 14b). Then he goes on to amplify this response: "For he says to Moses, 'I will have mercy on whom I have mercy, and I will have compassion on whom I have compassion' (v. 15)."

This is another example where Sproul ignores context and so inaccurately interprets the Scripture. Let's look at the passage to which he alludes:

> **Romans 9:14-16** *What shall we say then? Is there unrighteousness with God? Certainly not! For He says to Moses, "I will have mercy on whomever I will have mercy, and I will have compassion on whomever I will have compassion." So then it is not of him who wills, nor of him who runs, but of God who shows mercy.*

Here, Paul is quoting from Exodus 33:

> **Exodus 33:13-19** *Now therefore, I pray, if I have found grace in Your sight, show me now Your way, that I may know You and that I may find grace in Your sight. And consider that this nation is Your people." And He said, "My Presence will go with you, and*

> *I will give you rest." Then he said to Him, "If Your Presence does not go with us, do not bring us up from here. For how then will it be known that Your people and I have found grace in Your sight, except You go with us? So we shall be separate, Your people and I, from all the people who are upon the face of the earth." So the Lord said to Moses, "I will also do this thing that you have spoken; for you have found grace in My sight, and I know you by name." And he said, "Please, show me Your glory." Then He said, "I will make all My goodness pass before you, and I will proclaim the name of the Lord before you. I will be gracious to whom I will be gracious, and I will have compassion on whom I will have compassion."*

In context, God was not speaking of those to whom He would grant mercy because they called on the Name of the Lord and thus would inherit eternal salvation. He is speaking of restraining His judgment (having mercy/compassion) on some of the Jews who had worshiped the golden calf in Exodus 32, even though all who did so deserved to die immediately. **This passage is about *temporary physical* mercy, not eternal spiritual mercy/salvation.**

Most of the Israelites to whom God had shown temporary, physical mercy in Exodus 33 *fell under God's judgment* a few months later due to their disobedience, and they eventually died *without entering the Promised Land* (Numbers 14). In 1 Corinthians 10 and Hebrews 3-4, God makes it clear that *those who died in the wilderness did so in unbelief.*

Therefore, if the mercy of God in Exodus 33 was spiritual salvation mercy towards all who departed Egypt, then all those who were judged for disobedience (everyone over 20 years of age except Caleb, Joshua, Aaron and Moses) lost their spiritual salvation within a few months, an argument that Sproul would certainly not make.

When citing Exodus 33 in Romans 9, Paul is preserving the context to emphasize God's merciful character toward the unbelieving

Jewish people of Moses' day. Then, in Romans 11, Paul explains that even though the unbelieving Jews of his day had rejected Jesus as their messiah, this same mercy from God is what prevents Him from casting off the prophetic promises He made to the Jews pertaining to the last days.

> **Romans 11:19-27** *You will say then, "Branches [Jews] were broken off that I [Jewish/Gentile Church] might be grafted in." Well said. Because of unbelief they were broken off, and you stand by faith. Do not be haughty, but fear. For if God did not spare the natural branches, He may not spare you either. Therefore consider the goodness and severity of God: on those who fell, severity; but toward you, goodness, if you continue in His goodness. Otherwise you also will be cut off. And they also, if they do not continue in unbelief, will be grafted in, for God is able to graft them in again. For if you were cut out of the olive tree which is wild by nature, and were grafted contrary to nature into a cultivated olive tree, how much more will these, who are natural branches, be grafted into their own olive tree? For I do not desire, brethren, that you should be ignorant of this mystery, lest you should be wise in your own opinion, that blindness in part has happened to Israel until the fullness of the Gentiles has come in. And so all Israel will be saved, as it is written: "The Deliverer will come out of Zion, and He will turn away ungodliness from Jacob; for this is My covenant with them, when I take away their sins."*

In his final comment below, Sproul replaces the word "mercy" with "clemency." Why change from a word used in the Bible, "mercy," to the word "clemency"—a word that does not appear in English translations of the Bible because its equivalent is not used in the original language?

> R.C. Sproul – "Here the Apostle is reminding his reader of what Moses declared centuries before; namely, that it is God's divine right to execute **clemency** when and where

> He desires. He says from the beginning, *"I will have mercy on whom I will have mercy."* It is not on those who meet some conditions, but on those whom He is pleased to bestow the benefit."

I believe Sproul switches the word because clemency, although only slightly different in meaning, better supports the concept of a judge (in this case, God) reducing or eliminating a sentence that has already been adjudicated against an offender of the law. It therefore fits better with the Calvinist concepts of Original Sin / Total Depravity – that all souls are totally depraved and so condemned from the moment of conception; and Unconditional Election – that the Calvinist god forces some of those on death row to accept His **clemency**.

In contrast, mercy has both physical *and* spiritual relevance, allowing the reader to carefully discern from the context as to which one applies—while clemency applies only to the false teachings of Calvinism. We must be very wary of those who twist the Scriptures to support their doctrine.

Sproul states, "It is not on those who meet some conditions, but on those whom He is pleased to bestow the benefit."

On the contrary, however, Jesus makes it perfectly clear that there *is* a condition that people must meet for God to bestow the benefit of eternal life:

> **John 7:37-39** *On the last day, that great day of the feast, Jesus stood and cried out, saying, "If **anyone** thirsts, let him come to Me and drink. **He who believes** in Me, as the Scripture has said, out of his heart will flow rivers of living water." But this He spoke concerning the Spirit, whom **those believing in Him** would receive; for the Holy Spirit was not yet given, because Jesus was not yet glorified.*

This passage, and hundreds of others, refute the man-made, unbiblical, and false doctrine of Unconditional Election.

In summary, R.C. Sproul's proof text is a twisting of Romans 9:10-16, in the same way Calvinists twist Psalm 51:5 to come up with Original Sin; and thus, Total Depravity.

Limited Atonement

Limited Atonement is only needed because Total Depravity (as defined by Calvin) requires the capricious, Unconditional Election of those few that God chooses to save. It is inconsistent for the Calvinist god to send Jesus to die for the sins of people he knew he would never save, so he only died for the sins of those few that he randomly picks out of all humanity.

However, if the true God does not consider man to be Totally Depraved, and does not randomly elect those few to be saved but makes salvation open to any and all who would respond to the Holy Spirit and the preaching of the word of God, then His atonement is not limited, as the Scriptures make perfectly clear, only four of which are:

> **John 3:16-18** *For God so loved **the world** that He gave His only begotten Son, that **whoever** believes in Him should not perish but have everlasting life. For God did not send His Son into the world to condemn the world, but that **the world** through Him **might be** saved. "**He who believes** in Him is not condemned; but he who does not believe is condemned already, because he has not believed in the name of the only begotten Son of God.*

> **1 Timothy 2:3-7** *For this is good and acceptable in the sight of God our Savior, who desires **all men to be saved** and to come to the knowledge of the truth. For there is one God and*

*one Mediator between God and men, the Man Christ Jesus, who gave Himself **a ransom for all,** to be testified in due time, for which I was appointed a preacher and an apostle — I am speaking the truth in Christ and not lying — a teacher of the Gentiles in faith and truth.*

1 Timothy 4:9-11 *This is a faithful saying and worthy of all acceptance. For to this end we both labor and suffer reproach, because we trust in the living God, **who is the Savior of all men,** especially of those who believe. These things command and teach.*

2 Peter 2:1 *But there were also false prophets among the people, even as there will be false teachers among you, who will secretly bring in destructive heresies, even denying the Lord **who bought them**, and bring on themselves swift destruction.*

Limited atonement is a false teaching needed to support the false doctrine of Unconditional Election, which is needed to support the false doctrine of Total Depravity. As did Unconditional Election before it, the wall of Limited Atonement falls on the same foundation of sand that is Total Depravity.

Irresistible Grace

Irresistible Grace is essential if Total Depravity is true. We know that people are saved and are going to heaven. But Total Depravity teaches that it is impossible for the Totally Depraved person to hear, see, seek, repent, have faith, call upon the name of the Lord, etc. to become saved and justified in the eyes of a holy God.

> R.C. Sproul – "If, indeed, we are dead in sins and trespasses, if, indeed, our wills are held captive by the lusts of our flesh and we need to be liberated from our flesh in order to be saved, then in the final analysis, salvation must be

> something that God does in us and for us, not something that we in any way do for ourselves."

It is telling that R.C. Sproul did not use a single verse in his web posting on Irresistible Grace to support this tenet of Calvinism.

Why?

Because there is none.

The Scriptures are entirely silent on this unbiblical (and *extra-biblical*) concept of Irresistible Grace that R.C. Sproul summarizes this way:

> "In historic Reformation thought, the notion is this: 'regeneration precedes faith.' Other Calvinists use the phrase 'the person is born again before he/she can have faith to be saved.'"

When R.C. Sproul says, "If indeed, we are dead [as Calvinists define] in sins and tresspasses, if, indeed. . . ." he is admitting that Irresistible Grace is necessary to support their definition of Total Depravity.

But "if indeed" the Calvinist doctrine of Total Depravity is in error, then that would explain why God devoted *zero* inspired Scripture to support the notion of Irresistible Grace—and why Sproul is unable to find a single verse that he can twist to support this unbiblical doctrine.

Another wall of TULI collapses on the sandy foundation of Total Depravity.

Closing Thoughts

The Jews of the Old Testament did not read Psalm 51:5 as the Calvinists do. Neither did Jesus, the New Testament apostles, nor the early church until Augustine of Hippo in about A.D. 400 first taught this and other false teachings that have corrupted the church to this day.

The God of the Bible does not condemn babies or anyone else for the sins of others. He is a loving God Who seeks to reason with fallen, rebellious humans and calls on them to resist the lies of the first rebel, Satan. Scripture clearly teaches that when we are made aware of God's law, our rebel nature which we inherited from Adam will cause us to violate God's law and thus become a sinner. When we do sin, the wages of our actions at that moment is spiritual death—which is *eternal* separation from God.

> **James 1:14,15** *But each one is tempted when he is drawn away by his own desires and enticed. Then, when desire has conceived, it gives birth to sin; and sin, when it is full-grown, brings forth* **death** *[i.e., spiritual separation from God].*

But God so loved us that He provided a way to be delivered from darkness (sin and its consequences) into the light of the gospel, if we humble ourselves and respond to His offer of salvation:

> **James 4:7-10** *Therefore submit to God. Resist the devil and he will flee from you. Draw near to God and He will draw near to you. Cleanse your hands, you sinners; and purify your hearts, you double-minded. Lament and mourn and weep! Let your laughter be turned to mourning and your joy to gloom.* **Humble yourselves** *in the sight of the Lord, and He will lift you up.*

Galatians 3:24 *Therefore the law was our tutor to bring us to Christ, that we might be justified by faith.*

Hebrews 11:6 *But without faith it is impossible to please Him, for he who comes to God must believe that He is, and that He is a rewarder of those who* **diligently seek** *Him.*

I pray this booklet will help the saved person to look at every soul as someone who God loves and wants to save. With this biblical heart of a New Testament ambassador, you will be filled with a love for the lost and implore them to humble themselves before God (because they can). Tell them they need to turn away from their rebellion against God while there is still time. Plead with them to confess to God that they have sinned against their Creator and tell them they must call upon the name of the Lord Jesus for forgiveness and salvation. I invite you to join me in exhorting people to change from Calvinist clichés to biblical truth. Don't let people get away with saying, "We were born with original sin" or "a sin nature", or the related, "We sin because we are sinners", etc.", because they are not true.

I also pray that this booklet will help the unsaved person who has been written off by your Calvinist friend who has shrugged their shoulders and given up on you because you are obviously not one of the elect and therefore destined to hell. You are not unelected by God yet, because you are still alive. As the Scriptures make clear, God does not desire that any should perish, but that the sinner turn away from his wicked ways and be saved.

Romans 10:8,9 *But what does it say? "The word is near you, in your mouth and in your heart" (that is, the word of faith which we preach): that if you confess with your mouth the Lord Jesus and believe in your heart that God has raised Him from the dead, you will be saved.*

I have a heart-felt prayer for my Calvinist friends and those in the Calvinist camp who are reading this. As stated earlier, I exhort you to put down your books by Augustine, Piper, Sproul, Pink, Washer, et al., and just open your word-for-word translation of God's Holy Word, the Bible (KJV, NKJV, etc.) and ask God to reveal His truth to you on this matter. Don't let your mind insert parenthetical statements that are not there and don't belong. For example:

> **John 3:14-16** *And as Moses lifted up the serpent in the wilderness, even so must the Son of Man be lifted up, that whoever* (only the few God has elected to be saved) *believes in Him should not perish but have eternal life. For God so loved the world* (only the few God has elected to be saved) *that He gave His only begotten Son, that whoever* (only the few God has elected to be saved) *believes in Him should not perish but have everlasting life.*

> **John 11:25,26** *Jesus said to her, "I am the resurrection and the life. He who believes in Me* (only the few God has elected to be saved), *though he may die, he shall live. And whoever lives and believes in Me* (only the few God has elected to be saved) *shall never die. Do you believe this?"*

Stop looking at the masses of lost souls around you as pawns capriciously manipulated by God on His chess board of life, with most to be damned to the Lake of Fire and a few to be saved no matter what you try to do to reach them or they do in seeking God (because you have been falsely taught that they can't seek).

A Calvinist friend of mine went to the mission field in Thailand years ago. After helping to send him out, I found out that he had been converted to TULIP and Replacement Theology* and was teaching this to his students in Thailand. The consistent Calvinist would logically shun the mission field since the destiny of every soul on earth has already been determined apart from any efforts

---

* Replacement theology (also called supersessionism or fulfillment theology), is a false teaching held by Roman Catholics and many evangelicals which claims that the universal Christian Church has superseded the nation of Israel and therefore assumes (or "replaces") their role as God's covenanted people. This false doctrine leads to a host of aberrant beliefs and eschatological errors.

by man. I asked him why, considering his five point beliefs, he was on the mission field. He admitted that his efforts had no bearing on the eternal destination of those he was preaching to but he was going through the motions because that is what Jesus said to do. We then stopped our support for him and are praying his teaching will be thwarted by others who know their Bible and the true God of the Bible.

I encourage the Calvinist reader to get on your knees and ask God to help you be a laborer for the harvest, with a heart that the preaching of the gospel can truly impact the lives of sinners who humble themselves. The Bible teaches that saving faith comes by hearing—and hearing by the Word of God. That is why Jesus taught the gospel and exhorted us to do the same.

> **Matthew 9:36-38** *But when He saw the multitudes, He was moved with compassion for them, because they were weary and scattered, like sheep having no shepherd. Then He said to His disciples, "The harvest truly is plentiful, but the laborers are few. Therefore pray the Lord of the harvest to send out laborers into His harvest."*

Finally, I pray that this booklet will help true Christians refute those who hate God because they see the Calvinist god as a capricious, unloving, sadistic god that could have saved most but decided to save only a few. A god who does not allow (in his sovereignty) angels and man to have free will would make him responsible for the fall of Satan and Adam/Eve and he has therefore willed all the suffering of man throughout history.

If this is the god of the universe, then it is perfectly understandable why many unbelievers and atheists reject this perverted faith and wish to have nothing to do with it. But this is not the God of the Bible, and I pray this booklet can help you convince them that they need to read the Word of God for themselves, rather than rely on books or Youtube teachings by man. If they do, they will discover that the Bible teaches about a God Who created angels and man with an independent free will.

Without free will, there is no true love, but only robotic compliance, with most robots sent to the furnace. The biblical Jesus is the God of love and He is inviting all who will listen and respond to His invitation to come out of their sinful world and join Him in a restored loving relationship if they confess and receive His Grace and forgiveness, thus opening the door to everlasting life in heaven.

> **Matthew 11:28-30** *Come to Me, all you who labor and are heavy laden, and I will give you rest. Take My yoke upon you and learn from Me, for I am gentle and lowly in heart, and you will find rest for your souls. For My yoke is easy and My burden is light."*
>
> **1 John 4:7-11** *Beloved, let us love one another, for love is of God; and everyone who loves is born of God and knows God. He who does not love does not know God, for God is love. In this the love of God was manifested toward us, that God has sent His only begotten Son into the world, that we might live through Him. In this is love, not that we loved God, but that He loved us and sent His Son to be the propitiation for our sins. Beloved, if God so loved us, we also ought to love one another.*
>
> **Revelation 21:3-8** *And I heard a loud voice from heaven saying, "Behold, the tabernacle of God is with men, and He will dwell with them, and they shall be His people. God Himself will be with them and be their God. And God will wipe away every tear from their eyes; there shall be no more death, nor sorrow, nor crying. There shall be no more pain, for the former things have passed away."*
>
> *Then He who sat on the throne said, "Behold, I make all things new." And He said to me, "Write, for these words are true and faithful." And He said to me,*
>
> *"It is done! I am the Alpha and the Omega, the Beginning and the End. I will give of the fountain of the water of life freely to him who*

thirsts. He who overcomes shall inherit all things, and I will be his God and he shall be My son.

But the cowardly, unbelieving, abominable, murderers, sexually immoral, sorcerers, idolaters, and all liars shall have their part in the lake which burns with fire and brimstone, which is the second death."

Revelation 22:17-20 *And the Spirit and the bride say, "Come!" And let him who hears say, "Come!" And let him who thirsts come.* **Whoever desires,** *let him take the water of life freely.*

For I testify to everyone who hears the words of the prophecy of this book:

If anyone adds to these things, God will add to him the plagues that are written in this book; and if anyone takes away from the words of the book of this prophecy, God shall take away his part from the Book of Life, from the holy city, and [from] the things which are written in this book.

He who testifies to these things says, **"Surely I am coming quickly."** *Amen. Even so, come, Lord Jesus!*

Maranatha!

www.ingramcontent.com/pod-product-compliance
Lightning Source LLC
Chambersburg PA
CBHW071408040426
42444CB00009B/2144